# Facts & Arguments

## Selected Essays from
## THE GLOBE AND MAIL

EDITED BY

MOIRA DANN

PENGUIN
CANADA

PENGUIN CANADA
Published by the Penguin Group
Penguin Books, a division of Pearson Canada, 10 Alcorn Avenue, Toronto, Ontario,
Canada M4V 3B2
Penguin Books Ltd, 80 Strand, London WC2R 0RL, England
Penguin Putnam Inc., 375 Hudson Street, New York, New York 10014, U.S.A.
Penguin Books Australia Ltd, 250 Camberwell Road, Camberwell, Victoria 3124,
Australia
Penguin Books India (P) Ltd, 11, Community Centre, Panchsheel Park,
New Delhi – 110 017, India
Penguin Books (NZ) Ltd, cnr Rosedale and Airborne Roads, Albany, Auckland 1310,
New Zealand
Penguin Books (South Africa) (Pty) Ltd, 24 Sturdee Avenue, Rosebank 2196,
South Africa

Penguin Books Ltd, Registered Offices: 80 Strand, London WC2R 0RL, England

First published 2002

1 3 5 7 9 10 8 6 4 2

Manufactured in Canada.

NATIONAL LIBRARY OF CANADA CATALOGUING IN PUBLICATION DATA

Facts & arguments : selected essays from The Globe and mail / Moira Dann, editor.

ISBN 0-14-301330-0

I. Dann, Moira, 1957- II. Title: Facts and arguments.

AC8.F23 2002      081      C2002-903270-9

Visit Penguin Books' website at **www.penguin.ca**

# CONTENTS

# INTRODUCTION

Lots of readers take a back road into The Globe and Mail.

Many people tell me the Facts & Arguments page is the first thing they read in their weekday Globe and Mail; a select few confess to reading the paper completely in reverse, starting with what many call simply "the back page." It is, after the front page, the most-read page in the paper. Some call it "the people's page."

Facts & Arguments first appeared June 12, 1990, the brainchild of then-editor-in-chief William Thorsell, with quotidian guidance from brilliant editor Phil Jackman. Meant as an arena for lively reader debate similar to its Russian namesake, *Argumenti i Fakti*, readers soon transformed its essays into a forum for "personal, not political" discourse.

The page has also featured, since day one, the Social Studies column by Michael Kesterton, "a daily miscellany of information" culled from sources worldwide and showcasing drawings by award-winning editorial cartoonist Brian Gable.

In addition, the page has sometimes hosted Fifth Column-ists such as Jan Wong and John Allemang, and for the last number of years, Facts & Arguments has offered Lives Lived, obituaries written by people who knew the deceased that reach beyond funeral-home cliché.

The main event, though, is the page's centrepiece: the essays that have appeared five days a week on the Facts & Arguments page for more than 10 years. They have transcended rant, diatribe and sentimentality to become a startlingly accurate barometer of Canadians' concerns. A wet finger in the wind, if you will, of whatever idea-zephyr might be floating across the country. While the rest of The Globe apprises us of the world's backroom, boardroom and battlefield events, the Facts & Arguments page offers an idea of what's going on in the coffee rooms: what's stuck in the reader's craw and what's on the minds of Canadians.

They have been funny: On the road, a mom pulls over and takes her two hungry little sons to a restaurant with a friendly owl on its sign. They all pile inside before she realizes it's a Hooters (*Life lessons learned on vacation*, p. 264).

Many are poignant: A grown son visits and reads to his blind mother every night and listens to memories he triggers; she continues to live alone in her own home (*Reading for my mother in the evenings*, p. 6).

A few have been shocking to some: A mother considers how to explain sex toys to her wee daughter after the pre-schooler finds mum's purple vibrator (*My children meet Mr. Purple*, p. 41).

And still others are charming, quiet and subtly well-observed: A woman who parts with some notions about herself when she sells her never-played accordion at a garage sale (*Accordion dreams in the park on a Saturday*, p. 285).

We get close to 500 submissions some weeks and I have learned much about readers who take the time to craft something to submit: Canadians love to reminisce. They love their cats and dogs and rabbits and fish; their children and their parents are an endless source of love, frustration, learning and laughter. They love gardening and word-play. They are moved by the nation's landscape and their own sense of place in the country and in the world.

But what I've found most compelling about this job is how people can turn the kaleidoscope through which they view life, assume a fresh viewpoint and actually come up with a new idea. Not necessarily a big new idea, but something that challenges previous assumptions: an unusual new juxtaposition of several old ideas.

Readers often ask me what I look for beyond 800 to 1,000 words that are "personal, not political." I equivocate, not wanting to narrow the conduit and possibly preclude the submission of something startling, something I didn't even know I was looking for. But, if pressed, I will quote Rust Hills, former editor of fiction for Esquire magazine, who said: All you need to be a good writer is originality of perception and utterance.

Oh, is that all. It sets the bar kind of high, but so what? Many Facts & Arguments writers have soared over it seemingly without effort. And I believe they will continue to do so.

I'd like to thank: Previous F&A editors Phil Jackman, Constance Schuller and Katherine Ashenburg. My boss Patrick Martin and all my Comment section colleagues, particularly Dave Watson. Globe and Mail Deputy Editor Sylvia Stead for championing this project. Elaine Knapp and Ellen Keating for helping me contact writers. The monstrously talented illustrators who have provided the evocative art that is a hallmark of Facts & Arguments. Everyone who said, "Hey, great idea!" when they heard about the concept for this book. And Diane Turbide, Penguin Editorial Director, who agreed it was a great idea and made it happen.

But my biggest thanks go to the Facts & Arguments writers. The willingness of so many to utter their percep-tions is what's made the back page a listening post for the rest of us.

And to the readers of Facts & Arguments: It's an honour to have so many of you turn to the back first.

Moira Dann
Editor
Facts & Arguments

# FAMILY

# I'VE FINALLY BECOME SCARLETT O'NEILL

On Sunday mornings, when I was a little girl, I waited eagerly for the satisfying thump on the front porch that signalled the arrival of the weekend newspapers. We lived near a big city so there were two of them, the News and the Free Press; consequently there were piles of paper to go through—magazine sections, news, advertisements and, best of all, the coloured comics. (A news junkie to this day, I attribute my addiction to that early exposure.)

As the only child, I got first dibs on the comic sections. Each week, the adventures of my favourites unfolded in front of my eyes as I sprawled on the floor, surrounded by the papers, inhaling the faintly alkaline smell of newsprint. I never thought to wonder why Prince Valiant's perfect blunt-cut pageboy haircut was always clean and shiny even in the midst of the medieval battlefield, or how the fabulously red-haired Brenda Starr, Girl Reporter, saw through the star-shaped corneal openings of her eyes. Square-jawed Dick Tracy fought evil with no time to go to the orthodontist, and he assumed the favours of his faithful girlfriend

2

Tess Trueheart with never a lustful thought or action to betray his sole focus on fighting crime.

It did occur to me to wonder why L'il Abner never fastened the second strap of his overalls, or why his girl-friend Daisy Mae was barely clad at any hour of the day or night, but this seemed to be the Dogpatch way of life. After all, Dogpatch was also home to Sparkle Plenty, daughter of B.O., and a strange bloblike tribe of creatures called shmoos. L'il Abner's mother Mammy Yokum was abnormally stunted in growth due, no doubt, to the pipe permanently clamped between her teeth. But these absolute truths lay in the future.

All these favourites were only the appetizers. I always saved Invisible Scarlett O'Neill until the last. A girl detective, Scarlett could make herself invisible by pressing a nerve in her left wrist. In the invisible state, she could silently observe or do things for which she would never be held responsible. This all seemed very unlikely but no more so than the other characters.

An awareness of invisibility as a desirable state comes to most of us early on. Curiosity leads us to think how handy this could be and we learn to say, "I wish I could be a fly on the wall!" Although considering myself far too sophisticated to admit I believed this possible, I nevertheless took to groping surreptitiously along the inner hollow of my left wrist, looking for the mysterious nerve. What I would do when I found it was not really clear, but it had much to do with having the freedom to do what I felt like in any situation I chose.

As my life unfolded, I moved away from the city where I grew up, and the two Sunday papers ceased to be part of my weekly reading. I took to reading the New York Sunday Times on weekends. Ever more urbane, I now grabbed eagerly for the book reviews and ignored my old loves in the coloured comics. If I found myself thinking, "I wish I was a fly on the wall," it never occurred to me to grope my left wrist. I had grown up.

A few years ago, my wise friend Lorraine said thoughtfully to me, "You know, 60-year-old women are invisible." As this time was some years ahead of me, I merely tucked the idea away for future use.

Eventually, I, too, reached this landmark birthday (better than the alternative, as the saying goes). Although I had not particularly looked forward to this, I began to see possibilities. Being 60 and invisible is an emancipation.

The angst of my striving, competitive days was over. I could wear what I liked, think as I pleased and (mostly) say what I thought. Invisibility had descended as the proverbial cloak to cover me. Why did this state seem so familiar? Into my mind came the shadowy glimmerings of someone from my past. Why, it was Scarlett O'Neill herself! Although I could not remember exactly what she looked like, probably because she spent such a lot of time being invisible, many of my old dreams and fantasies of her advantageous ability came flooding back.

I tried out my new state in a conversation with someone who seemed not to see me as she talked away about her new hairstyle. "Oh, yes," I said, "that happened to me when I dyed my hair purple." No reaction, no response, and I gained courage. Perhaps she was just another self-centred conversationalist but the possibilities were there.

So far, I am not sure how far I want to go with this. But it's becoming more and more liberating. Don't know what to wear? Trapped in a boring conversation? I smile (to myself, of course—no one else can see me) and give my left wrist a little squeeze, and say or do whatever I please, more or less, given I've spent the greater part of my life as a responsible adult.

I don't want to spit on the sidewalk, or wear funny hats, but I like knowing I could if I wanted to.

The distresses of getting older are well-chronicled. But my joy of aging is in the freedom it gives. This is a special gift; I am not about to let it wither with disuse. I intend to work hard on nurturing the ability to have fun with it for a long time to come. The antique lady may be invisible. But she is smiling, and holding onto her left wrist. The thirty-something girl who lives inside me will gleam through, doing her own thing, just like Scarlett O'Neill.

*Vera-Lee Nelson*
Almonte, Ont.

# READING FOR MY MOTHER
# IN THE EVENINGS

Each evening after work, I walk the block and a half to the home where I spent most of my early life. I unlock the front door, turn off the alarm and call out a greeting to my mother.

It is something I have been doing almost daily for the past four years, since my father died.

If I get away early, by 4:30, I head for the kitchen, where Mom will be ladling a cup of "green soup" or "red soup" (named for the colour-coded plastic containers she has filled and frozen on her cooking day) over a one-third cup of grated cheddar cheese.

If I arrive closer to 5 o'clock, I sit down on the love seat next to her, lean over and give her a kiss on the cheek, and wait for her to finish her first course.

If it is 5:30, I am too late to perform my usual task, which is to take the bowl back to the kitchen and prepare dessert: One scoop of vanilla ice cream, half a banana from the refrigerator (sliced), and a crumbled cookie, all mushed together, with a spoonful of instant coffee "to keep me awake until 9 o'clock."

She sits patiently waiting for me to do this, and when I return, she takes two green pillows from beside her. One she places under her apron and uses as a small table, the other she hands me to rest my book upon.

And I begin to read.

We have read widely these past four years: Carol Shields and Bonnie Burnard, Timothy Findley and David Macfarlane, Odysseus and Gilgamesh, Genesis and Job, Elaine Pagels and Thomas Cahill, Annie Dillard and Lois Hole.

I have learned that "swear words" and references to sex will elicit disapproval, that complex plots are difficult to follow, and the Bible imprinted on her by twice-daily readings as a child is always an excellent area to explore.

I have also learned to recognize those places in my reading when my mother will interrupt, ask for a definition of a word or a geographic location, and send me (as she did when I was still at home) to pull down the Encyclopedia Britannica (bought in a Boston second-hand store in 1935 for $50) or heft up the foot-thick Webster's dictionary. One of these days, repetition will teach me the difference between Thomas à Becket and Thomas More. I have learned the derivation of the word "sycophant," although I didn't go into detail when I explained it to her. And I now know that Emily Dickinson (whose name, for reasons known only to Mom, kept intruding into our reading about Elizabeth Tudor) had a sister named Lavinia.

Often we make little progress in the current book. Something read, or something said, triggers a memory, and I will hear again some old familiar story. How as a student in high school, some 80 years ago, she first met my father at a St. Patrick's Day party and knew beyond a shadow of a doubt that he was to be her one true love.

How her father's father put his infant brother (the old man who gave me the cradle that I slept in as a baby, and that now my grandson sleeps in) up on the saddle in front of him and rode the quarter-mile down to the farm gate before handing him down and riding off to fight for the Confederate States of America.

Sometimes the story is new to me.

My telling her of cutting this year's Christmas tree brings a story of her childhood: how she, with her best friend, sent off in the buggy one summer's day to take some corn to the mill, sawed and hacked down, with rocks, a perfect evergreen. They took it home, and my grandmother (whom I remember clambering over the rail fence at the back of the property to take me berry picking) set the tree up in the yard and helped the two girls decorate it with popcorn strings.

When I am not there, more often than not she is "reading" one of the books sent her by the Canadian National Institute for the Blind. The CNIB book is sometimes a great frustration for her because the tape recorder is frequently out of adjustment and the book is often one in which she has little or no interest.

Some days, she spends most of her waking time preparing next week's meals, or doing last week's laundry. Although she has been quite blind for several years now (some slight peripheral vision remains), her memory guides her unerringly about the house. It is only when a crisis arises—the CBC has inexplicably shifted its location on the dial—that I am called to set things right.

After her dessert, if the weather is good, I walk slowly with her down my father's wheelchair ramp to the sidewalk. We take short steps, her hand resting in the crook of my elbow, and inevitably I think of the time, when I was considerably younger, I escorted my daughter down the aisle of St. Michael's Church.

When the weather is bad, we simply make the rounds of the main-floor windows, pulling down the blinds that signal to the neighbours that the evening has arrived.

Then I make sure the hall runner is pulled tight against the wall so she won't trip, turn on the lights in the bathroom and in my old main-floor bedroom, kiss her on her oh-so-soft cheek, hold her tightly to me for a quiet moment and stand outside on the porch while she locks the door behind me and signals through the glass that I can go.

*John M. Thompson*
London, Ont.

## THE WHEEL OF DEATH AND LIFE

The morning after, my mother says, "I don't know how else to tell you this, but your brother was killed last night on the QEW," as she leaves my cup of tea. I follow her upstairs and

ask if it was his fault. She doesn't know. She says she'll have
to pretend it didn't happen for awhile and goes into the
living room. We learn later that he was killed when a wheel
came off a truck and crashed into the roof of his Toyota
while he was on the way to his Monday night ball hockey
game.

My father is watching *Theodore Tugboat* with my daughter in the family room. He goes upstairs to write a memorial
for the funeral service that he recites to us. Our neighbour
appears on my parent's doorstep with a steaming lasagna in
his oven-mitted hands, tears streaming down his face. After
making the calls, I make a pot of coffee and pin the hem of
the skirt my mother is wearing to the funeral. We take it to
one of those quick-sew places and I want to tell the clerk
that it's for my brother's funeral. We buy navy-blue panty-
hose at The Bay.

When I see his picture on the front page of the newspaper, I think: good choice, his wedding picture, he's
wearing his glasses. It occurs to me that now only my
sister and I will be beneficiaries of my parents' estates. I sit
in a stupor on the couch while my husband reads the
announcement for the paper that re-names my newborn
son after my brother Jamie. He wants critical feedback,
but I can't give him any.

I remember not to wear mascara to the funeral. It's so
nice to see people from the past. We thank them profusely
for coming. I wolf down the casserole and the salad with
the poppyseed dressing brought over by the babysitter.

We are at the townhouse of my brother and his wife. His loafers stand in the front hall closet, as though expecting him. We rifle through his watches, belts and best shirts. I choose the Icelandic sweater I knitted for him and his tennis sweater. I smell them, trying to remember his aftershave. I want his university notes, for some reason I cannot fathom.

I industriously write thank-you notes and put the sympathy cards in a Tippet-Richardson box along with the newspaper clippings. I cross out "winter clothes" on the box and write "Jamie." There are lots of repeat cards; Hallmark should have a larger variety, I think. I let my daughter reach up to drop the thank-you notes in the mailbox. We swing on the tire at the park and she tells me she'll buy me a new brother.

There is a coroner's inquest into his death. In the room is the 200-pound wheel that killed him and a flipchart on which is written: "James Chester Tyrrell, date of birth Nov. 24, 1963, driving blue Toyota licence JLO 153, date of death April 3, 1995." I can't stop staring at the flipchart. We touch the wheel and the rusted screw that caused what the experts call a "wheel-off." There is a computer-generated animation of the accident showing exactly how and when the wheel struck the roof of his car. Everyone marvels at the technology. They mark colour photographs of his demolished car as "Exhibits." During the break, the cops and lawyers and victims go to the hotel lobby for coffee and joke around.

The nurse who was driving in the middle lane that night testifies. She tells us that when she got in the car, he was breathing but that it was just his reflexes, he was already dead. I lose my temper when the French translator for the truck driver who didn't realize he had lost a wheel makes a joke. "Do you find this funny?" I ask him. I want to punch in his loose-lipped mouth. The victim impact statement is read by my father, who says to the jury, "If you think you've had a hard time, try getting up every morning to bring your wife to this inquest." Afterwards we sit in Tim Hortons, trying to think of something to say.

Finally, the tears come. I cry in the car, I cry in the bathtub, I cry while I'm jogging. I cry like a baby, inconsolably.

It helps to rewind and replay; it wears the image down, makes it less vivid. My baby brother, *mon petit*, good guy, in his cut-off sweatpants, minding his own business, Rush in the tape deck. He always said he drove like an old lady, in the slow lane. Did he see the wheel, did he feel pain? This is the crucial question. No, I am told, his foot was still on the accelerator when the car finally came to a rest against the guard rail, almost a kilometre from where he was hit. What if he hadn't been in the slow lane or had to work late or missed the GO Train?

Mostly at night, I think about the hardest things: our family name ends here. He'll miss my parent's retirement years. No nephews or nieces for my children to play with. My son will never talk to his uncle Jamie about being a C.A. One less card on Mother's Day. No Toyota in the driveway at the cottage on Friday night. It will never be his message on my voicemail.

Things are better now, my mother's wearing makeup again; I don't hate everybody who got to live anymore and my Dad uttered my son's name last Sunday. I no longer tell strangers and check for their reaction. I have forgiven the woman who asked how long he lived after he was struck and the friends who left messages on my answering machine telling me to call if I needed anything.

It is more bearable now, a pang when I see a young man in the subway with a slightly receding hairline, a twinge waving to his best friend the other day as he was going for coffee with the guys from work, a little stab when I overheard my husband talking on the phone with his sister the other night. Needle pricks, compared with before. I can tolerate cracks at work about dying and walk by the last place we had lunch, Cultures, without ruining my day. But I still don't like lasagna and I can't take his business card out of my card case, or scratch out his name in my address book. And I'm still scanning the obituaries in The Globe and Mail most mornings, looking for people who died young.

I've heard that tragedy makes you kind. I am not so afraid anymore, of a car accident on the way to the video store, or when my parents leave to drive to Florida. What will be will be. I no longer feel obliged to thank God. I don't worry about losing a job or not paying a mortgage anymore, as long as no one else dies. I don't care who has more than I do. I don't fight with my husband very much.

I love my kids. I feel lucky. God's sac-fly. Maybe I feel punched out. Nothing really matters, except living.

*Laura Tyrrell*
Toronto, Ont.

## THE SISTERHOOD OF MISCARRIAGE

So here's what happened: Last summer, with my daughter Bonnie just under two years old, my husband, Alec, and I planned to start our second baby. We quickly became pregnant and celebrated the positive pregnancy test at the cottage in mid-August.

In mid-September, I lost the baby. (I have searched and searched for a phrase to describe this—"I had a spontaneous abortion," "I had a miscarriage," even "we discovered the fetus had failed to develop properly." But it is losing a baby, a tiny one, just two centimetres long.)

We were wrecked. Ship-wrecked, really. I never thought it could happen to us. We knew other people who'd had miscarriages, we knew other couples who couldn't get pregnant and, particularly after Bonnie was born, I ached for them. But I was also smug—we had a lovely pregnancy; a large, healthy baby; an amazing, physical, verbal genius of a toddler. We were okay.

So we went through all the crap necessary to "complete the abortion." I bled for two weeks. I had three ultrasounds. Adamantly opposed to a D & C, I finally took misoprostal suppositories to finish things off. And I cried and cried.

And then . . . then, I discovered the sisterhood of miscarriage. Absolutely everyone had had one. Four colleagues at work, three friends with children Bonnie's age, my mother, my sister, their friends. My mother's cousin, who had one child, three miscarriages and two more children. A friend who lost her first baby at 10 weeks and her second at 20. Another who had an ectopic pregnancy, then a miscarriage at 12 weeks (just when you begin to think you're safe).

So I learned from them. I learned there's always somebody worse off than you are. (Imagine not being able to get pregnant at all.) I learned to talk about it, because friends will share their pain with you and make yours less that way. I learned from my wonderful midwife, who called me every day for two weeks with an offering from her 15 years of experience. She said, "If a pregnancy is strong, you can't kill it with a brick; and if it's not, *you can't save it*."

And that was the hardest thing to learn—that there is nothing you can do. That one miscarriage—one "loss" as the medical profession calls it—is regarded as normal. One in five women have them. As many as half of all pregnancies end this way in the first trimester. And it's better that they do, because it almost always means the baby isn't developing properly. People said, "Mother Nature is taking care of you. You'll be fine next time,

don't worry." My sweet nephew told me the baby had
gone back to Heaven and was just waiting for a better
body next time around.

And we believed them. We waited the prescribed two
normal menstrual cycles and we tried again. And we got
pregnant easily, as always, and we were cautiously happy
about it; we didn't tell anyone right away; we passed the
eight-week point and I began to think it would be okay. I
convinced myself this pregnancy felt different, normal,
"More like it was with Bonnie." I was growing big, I had
morning sickness, everything was fine. And have you
noticed I'm using the past tense? Because I was wrong.

It happened again. Just two months ago, in fact. Alec
and I are waiting to see a specialist in "repeated loss." He
will tell us what "investigations" are "appropriate" for us. I
have collected my medical records to send to him. I have
done research on the Net—I have found several articles
outlining causes of repeated miscarriage. And none of it
helps, because I lost the baby again.

My husband and I went to the X-ray and ultrasound
lab together. We sat in the waiting room, knowing the
news was bad, surrounded by people and illness, and he
said to me, "Think of all the worse reasons for being
here." True.

My sister said, "But now you can do something—you can
see this specialist and find something out. Maybe there's
treatment. Maybe at least he can rule some things out. You
can know more next time."

True.

My midwife said, "You're under 37. You have no problem getting pregnant. You have regular menstrual cycles. And you have had a live birth already. Those are all things in favour of you succeeding with another pregnancy." True.

And none of it helps, because I lost the baby again.

I tried to explain it to Alec, this empty sense of loss. I said, "It's not that there's anything missing from our life—I have you, you have me, and we're wonderful. And we have Bonnie, and she has us, and she's amazing. And there's nothing incomplete there, there's nothing that needs fixing . . . but I want more of it."

"Yes," he said, "I want more *us*."

And that's it. It's the urge, the passionate, flaming desire, to create more *us*.

To give Bonnie a brother or a sister. To give Alec another child, another being in the world with some of him in it. To give all those mothers and mothers-to-be in the sisterhood of miscarriage another good-news story and a happy ending to help them along their way.

To give me, in some way, my two lost babies back.

So we will try again. The odds—just barely—are still with us. And we're young. And Bonnie is amazing.

And I just don't know what I'll do if we don't make it this time.

*B. Simmons*
Toronto, Ont.

# NEVER HERE, BUT NOT FORGOTTEN

On the 12th of November, I always think about my sister. Today is the anniversary of her birth, and her death. My sister died two years before I was born and nine years before my brother came along.

Stillbirth. To be born still. As a word, it is utterly inadequate to describe the death of a child at the moment of its birth. No one knows what to make of it or what to say. There were no doubt the platitudes from the well-meaning: "You're young. You can have another one" . . . "At least you never got to know her" . . . "She must have been so special that God wanted her back."

And, of course, the doctors told my mother that this was Nature's way of protecting us, that there must have been such serious problems that, had she lived, she would surely have been disabled. A blessing, really.

"She could have had two heads," my mother has always told me. "I couldn't have loved her more." She was my sister, my mother has always told me, and her name was Sheila.

My mother was only 22 years old when she went into labour with her first-born, and she was all alone. My father was stationed in Nairobi, Kenya, with the British army and had used up all his available leave in the months leading up to his child's birth, coming home to Scotland to visit his ailing father and ultimately for his funeral.

Still, my mother found a way to feel his presence and to help him feel that he had been there. She wrote a long letter to him throughout her labour, sharing with him her fears, her excitement and her joy. At some point, she stopped writing and went to the hospital.

Although this was her first baby, she sensed that things were not going well—that something was, in fact, going terribly wrong. She was given a little bell to ring when she was ready. None of the hospital staff took her concerns seriously. She was left alone.

It was several hours later that the emergency was recognized by the professionals, hours that must have been unbearable for my mother and were a lifetime to my sister. My mother was quickly anesthetized. When she awoke, glad it was all over and anxious to meet her baby, no one would answer her questions. When she asked desperately to see her baby, nurses walked away from her without a word.

Finally, she was told that her beautiful daughter had died at birth, the umbilical cord having been wrapped around her neck. In retrospect, they told her, the trouble she sensed had, in fact, been the baby struggling to be born, held back by the noose around her little neck. Probably due to a fall my mother had taken during her fifth month, she was told.

My mother never saw her daughter, but they told her she looked perfect, with dark hair, 10 fingers, 10 toes. The only tangible evidence my parents had of the little girl's existence was the funeral home bill, detailing the cost of disposal of this precious life.

I ache for my mother every year on Nov. 12 and feel this protective anger toward those who acted with such a lack of compassion toward her. After learning of her baby's death, she was moved into one of those 1950s megawards along with nearly a dozen other women and their babies and their husbands.

She was left alone, again, to express her milk and suppress her pain: It wouldn't have been right to upset the others, who were so hormonal and so happy.

On the base just outside of Nairobi, my father was a communications officer. He was off duty but raced back to receive the incoming message from his wife, anxious to know if he had a son or daughter. He listened, dot by dot, to the Morse code message and at some terrible moment he must have realized its meaning. It was only when I had my own baby that my father talked about the devastation of their loss.

But he has never spoken of that moment of knowing.

Although my sister's time here lasted such a brief moment, her presence has endured. She has always been a part of our family. In fact, in Grade 6, I created an entire life for her, telling my friends about my older sister, who attended another school, played the saxophone in the school band and wore a bra. Luckily, we moved just as my friends began asking to meet her.

We have always imagined her. And every year on Nov. 12 we try to do something special for my mother as she works her way through her grief even 43 years later. My parents have kept the spirit of this child alive in our family, giving her short life meaning.

And while we have not had the actual experience of her, we have had the sense of her. In our hearts and minds, she has had birthdays and boyfriends, sad times and happy times and, for a while, at 13, she played the saxophone.

*In loving memory of Sheila Ann Johnston—Nov. 12, 1958, to Nov. 12, 1958.*

*Cherished daughter of Bill and Sheila, sister of Karen and Bill.*

Karen Kirkconnell
Guelph, Ont.

## THE LURE OF TACKLE

With chubby, determined hands, my young son sorted and organized his grandfather's collection of lures every summer at our cottage in Ontario, on a quiet Muskoka lake.

In my son's imaginary world, a Crazy Crawler could morph into a spinning emerald insect with giant black wings. The Daredevil could transform into a red-and-white spiral rocket. A transparent green bug, the River Runt Spook Sinker, could shoot out a silver tongue at any passing enemy.

Mystical creatures with unique personalities, the best lures have reptilian features, strange appendages and glowing scales. They wiggle in the water, dance merrily at the tug of a rod and spin their metal tails with bubbly abandon.

My son discovered the lure of tackle as he played patiently on that cottage dock.

Inspirations for imagination, the lures beckoned him to journey beyond the majestic pines, granite rock and rippling water of Kapikog Lake.

My father's impressive jumble of lures has become a treasured family keepsake. With a July birthday, he had accumulated a formidable stash of tackle from our well-meaning family.

Every summer, I grazed the aisles of the local hardware store in search of the perfect gift. New fishing rod? No, too expensive. New hammer? No, too much work. New fishing lure? Yes, the right price for my meagre budget and, by gosh, I knew for sure that he would like it.

I must have had very lofty ambitions for the fishing potential on our small lake. The chosen lures were selected for their colour (the brighter, the better) and the size (the bigger, the better). What fish could resist an Arbo Gaster, glimmering with gold metallic paint, jet-black spots, bulging yellow eyes and a shredded rubber tail?

My father would smile benevolently with every gift given. "That one looks like a winner." The new lure was always given a preferred home in the top, pop-out tray of the tackle box.

Each lure had a chance for a life of glory. Surefire lures were bound for hard-working duties, always on hand to glide into the water at the best fishing spots. Lures with less-than-stellar performances were relegated to a mangled heap in the bottom of the box beside cracked bobbins and snapped lines.

My son patiently untangled each lure, one by one.

Deftly bypassing the minefield of jagged hooks, he seized a Canadian Wiggler with a triumphant grin. What living creature possesses a sleek orange body with red spots and black stripes?

"What's this?" Salamander? Frog? Newt? Centipede?

"What's this?" My son's eyes were saucer-shaped, baiting me to come up with the correct scientific identification.

So, as each lure was set free, I squinted at the names printed on their bellies: South Bend Super Duper, Rapala Wobbler, Beno—my son echoed those words with clear acceptance and seeming understanding.

The lures escaped their tangled heap and took their rightful place on the weather-worn wooden dock. The clawed crayfish were set together, and lures with propeller noses were matched snout to snout. Truly unique individuals, such as the Brooks Reefer, with a platypus head and webbed tail, were allowed to rest on solitary thrones of sunlit pine cones.

When my son was old enough to hold a fishing rod, my father would buckle up his pint-size fluorescent orange life-jacket and together they would set off across the lake.

With the small motor humming, the skiff would glide through the sparkling waves and pause in shallow coves along the far shore.

The brightness of their smiles was directly linked to the success of their fishing expedition. Never mind that all fish were returned, after jubilant cries, to the water. The happiness was in the journey, not in the catch.

Now a teenager, my son has no interest in fishing. Absorbed in the visionary world of video games and sci-fi movies, strange life forms lure him to imaginary places, like a toddler mesmerized with the discovery of lizards, insects and amphibians.

When my father passed away several years ago, I was not able to bring myself to toss out the vintage remains of his cottage pastimes.

His tackle box was shifted to the back of the waterside storage shed, alongside his beaten-up deck shoes, ancient rusty tools and tin cans full of nails.

Like the last breath of summer determined to linger on past the glowing hints of autumn, that tackle box remained in a dusty corner until this year. I hauled it down to the dock, clicked the plastic latch and lifted the lopsided lid. A rush of memories flooded over me when I saw the pile of hooked lures.

There are many lessons to be learned, about patience and imagination, in a tackle box.

*Jane Cline Rubicini*
Kitchener, Ont.

## HOLDING IT TOGETHER
## BY LIVING APART

My husband and I have a fairly happy marriage. It's had ups and downs as in most partnerships, but we have made it through 19 years together and that, I feel, is something nowadays. I like to think that one reason we have made it so far is the fact that we don't live together anymore. We are a weekend couple.

No, not long-distance: We don't live in different cities. We just live in different neighbourhoods. It takes me a 20-minute walk to get to my husband's bachelor apartment. Are we nuts? According to some people, certainly, although not everybody who knows us knows of our strange living arrangement.

We have been living separately for four years. It all began five years ago when our marriage started falling apart. We were openly discussing divorce but then decided to give it a last chance. Some time out, some space and distance. What was meant to be a temporary measure turned into a long-term solution. Needless to say, we don't have children. So we are able to indulge in this luxury of maintaining two small, no-frills households.

I won't bore you with all the details of why we were at the verge of marriage breakdown. Certainly the pressure of recent immigration, of not having a strong supportive network of friends and relatives around us, a new language and culture, floating in and out of the job market: these all played their parts.

Also, my husband and I have different notions of order. My husband's dis-order involves a system of piling papers, books, bills, receipts and all kinds of important documents onto and into each other, and then stuffing them all together in, on or under major pieces of furniture, which periodically have to be emptied, moved or turned every time he has to find a particular paper right at that very moment. And then his urge to collect stuff, such as pieces of half-rotten wood (for later woodwork or reparations), old radios and partial TVs (that might be useful at some point in his life), rusty tools, old furniture, tattered books and broken cutlery. Call him a living recycling machine. Add to this his total refusal to accept my help to put order to his stuff. Now, picture this in a one-bedroom apartment.

Back home in Central America all this wasn't really a problem. We had a little house; there was a back and a front yard. I remember my husband hammering and sawing away under mango trees and banana plants. Collecting stuff then made sense because there was a shortage of virtually every-thing and I even washed and put away every plastic bag we could find. But here in Canada, in the small one-bedroom flat we had, with a well-stocked hardware store at every corner, this Third-World hamster complex became obso-lete and a complete nuisance.

My own sense of order, although far from being compul-sive or obsessive, involves traditional things such as labelled boxes, files and properly stuffed bookcases. I, too, collect lots of things. After coming to Canada, I became an enthusiastic quilter. I stack material of all colours and qual-ities, threads in every matching colour, cutting boards, rulers, needles, bags full of ribbons and laces, boxes of buttons, baskets with pieces of fabrics I don't dare to throw away because they might be useful someday. You see, we both need a lot of space. Living apart has solved this space problem, among others.

Let's talk snoring. I'm a light sleeper and not even earplugs can keep his rattling, roaring and barking out of my ear canal. Before, my nights consisted of sleeping for short periods of time, sitting up, trying to wake my husband, pinching his nostrils, sleeping 30 minutes, sitting up, adjusting the earplugs that had fallen out, trying to get back to sleep for another half-hour. This, I believe, is sleep deprivation, and outside the bedroom, it is considered to be quite effective for breaking prisoners' wills. All this is over now. My health and mood have improved greatly.

We haven't yet resolved the problem with my in-laws. They don't know. Thank goodness they live in Los Angeles and so far only two of his sisters have showed up (once) unexpectedly, calling from the airport and driving us into a frenzy of bringing some of his stuff over, rearranging my place so it would look more like our place. Fortunately, they stayed for only two days. Some deep-seated culturally conditioned embarrassment keeps us (him) from telling the truth and so we continue with this comedy.

Are there any disadvantages? You bet. Start with the financial part, such as paying for his bachelor and my one-bedroom apartments. Separate shopping, cooking, telephone. But when people mention it, I tell them, well, if we had not moved apart, we would have most probably separated for good. So we would be apart anyway.

There are moments in the evenings when I wish he were here. I sometimes sense the danger of growing apart, of developing two completely separate lives, of losing too much touch. Reality checks restore my confidence quickly. I just look around me and see once-happy and so-much-closer relationships dissolving back into singlehood.

And then, we do have a lot to talk about on the weekends. We date. We meet somewhere for dinner, go to the movies (and afterwards either to his or to her place) and catch up on the past week's events. There is a little element of newness back in the relationship. I am happy when he comes on Saturday and I am happy when he goes on Sunday. Do I worry about him cheating on me? Does he worry? To be honest, I don't. Neither does he. Without trust, you can't live apart. But then, without trust, you can't live together either, can you?

M. *Rodriguez*
Toronto, Ont.

## LESSONS PASSED THROUGH WINDOWS

There is a stranger waiting in our driveway when I return home. He sits patiently on an overturned white pail, but stands and smiles warmly when he sees my car.

I give him only a faint, polite smile in return, showing him the kind of insincere courtesy I might show the clerk at my local convenience store. I park my car and walk over to him, guarded, even a little suspicious; I do not know this man.

He's close to 40 years of age and wears sweatpants and a casual T-shirt. His hair is brown and wavy and frames a tanned, pleasant face. He's slim, but physically fit.

"Can I help you?" I ask, a twinge of hostility in my voice.

"Hi, is your dad home?" he replies kindly.

"No, he's not home from work yet," I answer, stolid, composed, still no real warmth in my voice.

Upbeat, he says, "Well, I'll just wait for him. He said he'd be home at about 5:30."

"Oh, okay, sure," I reply hesitantly.

I turn to walk into the house.

"I used to see your dad running in the park," he shouts.

"Oh yeah, that's great," I utter, still responding with empty enthusiasm, still treating him with the vacuous tone that is often reserved for bellhops or waiters in our society.

"I'll just wait here," he states happily as I go inside.

I watch from the front window as he sits contentedly on his makeshift chair, the sun beating down on him. And sure enough, at 5:30, my father's 1975 blue rusting Chrysler with duct tape affixed to a front headlight, pulls into the driveway.

My father jumps out of the car in his dusty, tattered clothes, and greets the man excitedly. They shake hands, like old friends.

"Glenn, how are you?" my dad quickly says.

"Good, Elliot, good; your son sure has grown."

"Yeah, I don't know where the time goes."

Glenn nods knowingly and grins. My dad smiles back and in silence, they share what must be a fatherly moment.

Then, my dad chimes in sincerely, "I hope you haven't been waiting long." It had been almost 45 minutes.

"No, no, don't be silly," Glenn retorts.

I had wondered many things about Glenn that day. Foremost among them was why he was waiting in my yard at a time when most men were at work. Then, Glenn started talking.

"Listen, I had some extra time after doing the windows, so I cleaned out the eavestroughs too. They were pretty full." He *was* working.

"I appreciate that, Glenn," my dad said kindly. "Come on inside, I'll just get my wallet."

Now the man was inside my house.

"You play basketball, don't you, son?"

"Yeah, how did you . . . ?"

"I remember watching you on the driveway last time I was here."

I pretend to remember. As my father hands Glenn some money, I realize that I never noticed him before.

Or maybe I did, but only in the way one notices the person sitting beside you on the subway, which is to mean that I never noticed Glenn in a meaningful way.

"Thanks, Elliot," Glenn said warmly.

"We'll see you next time," my dad said, inviting another visit soon. Glenn smiled appreciatively and gently closed the door behind him. I looked over at my father inquisitively.

"That was Glenn," he said. "He's a real nice man with a young family. Three kids."

I nod, understanding. Glenn was washing windows for his family.

I venture that the best lessons come from example and not from the serious talks that many fathers put so much weight on.

I remember my father sitting me down for a talk about the birds and the bees about a year and a half *after* I had begun learning about pollination and nesting; despite his attempt to be calm and collected, he came across as though he had been rehearsing his speech in front of my mother for weeks and still wasn't ready for opening night.

But action, that's another thing; he has only pleasantly surprised me with that.

As I watch Glenn walk away past my father's old, dilapidated car and see my dad unbutton his worn-out shirt, I realize that it is better to drive a car that costs much less than you can afford, to wear clothes again and again until they wear out, but to always, always, hire the window washer when he comes knocking on your door.

*Adam Rodin*
Winnipeg, Man.

## LOST AND FOUND

One day this spring, our youngest son was accidentally hit in the head with a baseball bat. Four days later, I lost my purse. The two events may not seem to be connected.

Though he immediately sprouted a blue-black egg at the top of his forehead, our son did not lose consciousness. Within four hours, he returned from the hospital to recuperate from a mild concussion. He was lucky. The doctor said that had he been hit just an inch lower, at the temple, he would have been medi-vac'd from our small town to a city trauma unit, or worse.

I spent the next few days marvelling at his youthful ability to bounce back quickly, at the fortunate placement of the unfortunate strike of the bat, and at how an inch can matter so much.

That same week, my son's first day back at school, we had a call from the marina informing us that our boat was sinking. I went down to take my shift at the bilge-pumping we needed to do until the mechanic could dry-dock the boat and fix it.

I unsnapped the boat's canopy to make a space to climb through. In a hurry, distracted, and full of the as-yet-unrecognized potential for human error to come, I loosened only a few snaps and began to squeeze myself through the space. Another snap, another few inches, and I might not have lost my purse. But in my attempt to get through what was an unrealistically small opening for a 5'9" woman nearing mid-life, I forgot momentarily that I was carrying it. As I struggled to pull my arm through, the purse got left behind, falling into the water and sinking.

When I realized what had happened, I knew it was too cold to swim, too deep for a shallow dive. My purse was gone. But, strangely enough, I did not panic. I did not even feel anger at myself or sadness at the loss. With a surge of practical calm, I turned the bilge pump on.

Juxtaposed against my son's near-tragedy, this event seemed cause for laughter. Worse things, I knew, could happen.

Human beings can be both enormously adaptable and exceedingly kind. Over the next few hours, I witnessed just how much.

The dock owner also runs a sandwich shop, and when I went to ask his advice about what to do, he offered me a free lunch while we brainstormed. I might not retrieve my purse, but I wouldn't go hungry.

I proceeded through my day with a spare car key, making calls and fielding helpful suggestions about how to locate someone with a dry suit who might be interested in an excursion beneath the docks. Everyone I talked to wanted to help and seemed willing to offer a new suggestion. Eventually, I located two professional divers with full oxygen tanks who said they'd be happy to do it. This seemed nothing short of a miracle.

Strangely enough, my initial feelings of merriment were never replaced with panic. I had to admit to feeling lighter somehow, for having lost the weight of that purse on my shoulder.

Purses and wallets contain an entire lifetime, really. Keys to homes, cars, cottages, garages, storage lockers. Credit cards, social insurance, birth certificates, driver's licences, shopping club memberships. Even family photos. Who we are, how we live, and what we value can all be charted through the inner landscape of a purse.

Well, *almost* all we value. When I met the divers at the
dock at 7 that night, they asked me what the purse looked
like, how heavy it was, if there was anything of value in it.
"Anything of value?" I responded. I thought about the
twinkle in my son's eye and the yellowish bruise on his
forehead. "No," I said. "Not really."

Purses and wallets connect us to our identities as material
beings. People who own things, live places, buy things.
Faced ever so briefly by a life without a purse, a life without
"things" and devoid of economic identity, I realized how
much what defines me materially can also limit me.

Purseless, I found my shoulders thrown back more easily.
I smiled widely at the memory of the generous sandwich as I
walked down the street. I thought about the comic value
hidden in most human error. And I thought about my son.

I am extremely grateful that our boat began to sink and
I lost my purse only a few days after my son's nearly tragic
accident. I have been reminded by this juxtaposition of the
limitations to happiness in the materially constructed
world around me, a world I participate in, to be sure. But I
know with new certainty that the real value of life does not
fit into a purse or wallet. The real value is a human one
which defies any attempt at quantification. Last night, I
watched my son rolling in a sand pile with his friends,
dirtying his clothes, filling his shoes with grit, making a
powerfully large mess. And I marvelled.

Yes, the divers found my purse, in just under a minute. Its
soggy, blurred contents are spread across my kitchen table

now, drying. Of course I will load the purse up and carry it again, but now with a different sense of its limited space. The heart, on the other hand, knows no bounds.

*Eileen Delehanty Pearkes*
Nelson, B.C.

## I AM MY BROTHER'S BEST DEFENCEMAN

August 29, 1995, was the day I first met my brother. What makes that remarkable was that he was 21 at the time and had lived most of his life in the same house as me. My life changed forever that day. So did his.

He told me he was gay.

Dale Robert Miller was born in October, 1974. My parents used to tell the same story year after year: Dale learned to run before he could walk. It was true. I'm three years older and I can't close my eyes and remember him ever standing still. He ran, he skipped, he did flips and he laughed. He had one of those perpetually sunny dispositions that annoy siblings and make parents ask you, "Why can't you be as pleasant as your brother?" We moved around a lot. Dad was in the RCMP and although Dale and I were both born in Winnipeg, by the time I was 12 we had moved eight times and we lived just outside Sydney, N.S.

Dale was in that follow-your-big-brother-no-matter-where-he-goes phase, and this pain was compounded by my mom's insistence that "you should include your brother more . . . he loves you."

Ugh. I was 12. Having a brother who loved me was not cool. Especially Dale. He was different. He didn't want to play baseball or road hockey or have spitting-for-distance competitions. Hell, he couldn't spit for crap. His sport was embarrassing me. When I would walk by the tennis courts to go play football with my friends, somebody invariably yelled, "Hey Miller, isn't that your sister, I mean brother?" Laughs all around. Dale loved to hang out and skip with the girls. Not skip class. Skip rope.

He'd sing the songs that the girls were singing to keep time, oblivious to the words hurled at him.

"Faggot!"

"Queer!"

"What are ya, a girl?"

His face would momentarily darken while he waited for his turn to skip, and then he'd smile and laugh as he enjoyed the child's ability to be immersed in the moment.

A week later he brought my humiliation to a new level.

I went to a school that was divided into two distinct halves. One side was for the little kids; the other, for big kids. I was playing ball hockey on the big kids' side, having just been newly promoted to a big kid myself and trying desperately to make the role fit.

"Hey Miller, your little fairy-god-brother's here."

I heard this kind of stuff all the time. I always let it go. There was Dale, red-faced, screeching my name and crying so hard that he'd started hiccuping between words. A kid I'll call Blair, a hard-ass 10-year-old, had punched Dale in the stomach and called him a faggot.

I was mad. But not because some punk punched my brother. I was mad because my overly sensitive brother was drawing attention to me to defend him for acting gay. I put my head down and walked to the little kids' side of the school. I spotted Blair and marched at him like a dog that you know is going to bite you.

"What did I do? I just tapped him in the gut. He was acting quee . . ." I grabbed him by the throat.

"You ever even look at him again and I'll kill you."

I stared at him until he looked like he understood—or at least until I could see the blood vessels in his eyes—and walked back.

Dale was already recovering with the school's monitor, who, coincidentally, we all assumed to be gay, but never said so because he had a grip that could separate your shoulder.

That was the first time I ever stood up for my brother for being called something homophobic. It was also pretty well the last time.

Dale became increasingly less sunny over the next several years. He stopped laughing. He started junior high, humourless. He left high school bitter and outright mean—at least from my family's perspective. Years later, I asked him about it. He said it had a lot to do with knowing he was different and knowing some people would hate him for it.

"Okay, I'm just going to say it," my brother told me in Ottawa in 1995. "I'm gay and I don't care what anyone thinks."

I didn't show it, but it was hard news to hear. I always knew it, I guess, but now it was definite. He was gay. (I'd just finished university and had graduated from small-town homophobe to the guy who'd say, "Hey, some of my friends are gay.")

"I know. That's fine," I said, and he was so happy he cried.

But I wasn't really telling the truth. I knew people who were gay and I didn't hang out with them. Cape Breton is known for a lot of things: beauty, music, unemployment. But being gay-friendly isn't high on the list. Like quite a few non-urban areas, it's not known for a lot of tolerance. I had been conditioned, to an extent, to believe that it just wasn't right to be gay. Just like I was socialized to believe that Protestants wouldn't get into the same posh neighbourhood in heaven as Catholics and that, no matter who a person is, if they voted NDP, they weren't quite right.

Now I was being forced to re-think everything I assumed about my brother: he actually did like guys more than girls; when they called him a fag, it was more than schoolyard meanness—it was an indictment.

It took months to get used to it. My girlfriend made it easier by phoning him and playfully telling him gay jokes, or asking him which guys were cute. After a year, I could tell people—guardedly. After two years I wanted people to tell me what it was like to be gay. I read about it. I watched TV programs on it. Now I don't even think about it. He's my brother, I love him and, oh yeah, he's gay and has heard enough crap about it for a lifetime.

I don't let it go anymore. When I hear homophobic stuff, I say something. I let people know that gay people don't deserve to be born hated.

An Environics poll tells us that, nationally, 34 per cent of Canadians disapprove of homosexuality. That's a big improvement from even five years ago when 48 per cent disapproved.

Canada is considered to be one of the most gay-friendly states in the world. But queer people still hear every day that they should be burned, killed, exiled—from regular people who fix our cars, manage our portfolios and deliver our mail.

I just hope that someday, they feel as bad as I do for not changing my mind earlier.

*Derek Miller*
Toronto, Ont.

# MY CHILDREN MEET MR. PURPLE

It's a lazy, hazy morning in the "family bed." My husband and I yawn our way into daybreak while our kids arrive to bounce and dance around us. Mommy and Daddy can still feel the effects of last night's pleasure-seeking tornado and find it excruciatingly painful to wake up.

The house is a mess and we just can't seem to face the day. The hedonistic winds of the night have swept their way through the house leaving a trail of clothes and empty wineglasses. A trail leading to . . . "Oh look," says my husband rather too cheerfully. "Benjamin has Mr. Purple."

And behold my two-year-old son has gleefully discovered my vibrator. The infamous sex-toy that Mommy forgot to hide away in the dark hours of the night.

And of course, my son has learned the multi-faceted nature of my dear purple pal much faster than I ever did. He has it on full-speed and it's turning, rotating and vibrating itself into being the centre of attention. It's his new Action Hero.

Stupefied, I struggle to find my maternal voice but it's two pitches higher than usual. Somehow I've instantly morphed from Courtney Love into June Cleaver, and in a rather squeaky, shaky voice, I say, "Oh, you can't play with that (dear), that's not for children."

My six-year-old-daughter immediately grabs the rotating monster from her brother and a stream of questions tumbles from her mouth. "Why can't we play with it? Why?! What is it?"

"Just give it back to me," I snap, while trying to pry the silicone beast out of her clenched hands. This tactic is definitely not working. The more I ignore her questions, the more demanding she becomes. It's not possible to simply take Good ol' Purple away from her and toss it in June and Ward's secret party stash. I say to myself: "Can I tell her the truth?"

I grew up thinking that I was the only child in the world who masturbated. I thought it was somehow harmful and felt it was my duty to rid myself of this "dirty" habit. Touching myself was a pleasure met with shame. And although I've learned to be a happy and healthy masturbator, it wasn't until I gave birth to my daughter that I found I could actually talk openly about the practice. And so last year, I was excited to produce a TV segment that exposed the roots of the long-standing taboo against female solo sex. I wanted to explore the stigma of sexual pleasure in our culture, talk about the history of masturbation in North America and show images of real women in today's world who are unashamed about masturbating.

I featured clips from Dr. Betty Dodson's self-loving classes. Considered to be the "Grandmother of masturbation," Dr. Dodson, who is an author and sex-educator, has taught self-loving and sexual consciousness-raising classes to women for the past 27 years. Many of the women who come to Dr. Dodson have never experienced an orgasm. And like me, Dr. Dodson believes that if women give themselves permission to have independent orgasms, they will have independent thoughts. They will be autonomous, sexually confident beings, who won't have to be sleeping beauties waiting for a prince to awaken them. If young girls knew where everything was and how to give themselves guilt-free sexual pleasure, they might not run out and have sex with the first guy that comes around.

So amidst interview clips from Dr. Dodson, the viewer glimpses a circle of vibrating, naked women of all different sizes, shapes and ages. "Squeeze and release," Dodson is saying with a beatific smile on her face. And the women, who are all standing, rock their pelvises to and fro, their enormous vibrators strategically placed between their spread legs, their heads thrown back in ecstasy. I thought the sight of these masturbating women was intriguing—even humorous. I kept thinking: How could we have come to a point in our culture where we actually have to have masturbation classes? How sad.

But to many of our viewers, the sight of masturbating women was, simply, disturbing. In the history of the show, we've never had so many complaints lodged against us as when we aired the female-masturbation segment. People actually lodged complaints to the governmental commission that regulates the television industry. And what's weird is that the show is called *Sex TV*. Compared to other stories that we've aired, the masturbation segment is downright wholesome. Even so-called "sex-positive" women in the "funky/cool" TV station where I work were shocked and disturbed at the sight of these women masturbating.

The fact is that we still live in a very pleasure-negative culture, and masturbation has absolutely no rationale except pleasure. The clitoris—being the seat of pleasure—has been the source of sin for many centuries.

And things haven't really changed that much. It was only in 1994 that Dr. Jocelyn Elders, U.S. Surgeon General, was "abruptly fired" by former President Clinton after saying that masturbation was part of human sexuality and should be taught in schools.

How ironic that Dr. Elders was fired for mentioning the words "masturbation" and "education" in the same sentence, while Clinton's popularity rose after the words "fellatio" and "president" were found on the front page of every newspaper in the world.

And so I'm helping to "out" masturbation from its repressive history. Masturbation is our sexual base. It's our sexual response pure and simple. Unharnessed and primal, it teaches us about what turns us on. It's because we masturbate that we are more likely to orgasm while making love to our partners. And it's because we touch our clitorises during penetrative sex that we can reach orgasm.

Mr. Purple is Mommy's best friend. She's been dear to mothers for decades. At that moment, I decide to tell my daughter that the purple object that she tightly clasps is an adult toy that Mommy uses to pleasure herself.

And my six-year-old looks me in the eyes, with a quiet awareness, and hands me back my vibrator. As if nothing had happened, she smiles and continues with her childhood adventures. And I let out a breath of relief, no longer fearful of the day when my children discover a weird purple object hidden in Mommy's chest of drawers.

*Michelle Melles*
Toronto, Ont.

## LIKE FATHER, UNRECOGNIZABLE SON

For most of my life, I thought my father had a first-class mind and a quiet confidence.

He could solve complex mathematical problems and design floor plans. With his hands, he could do wonders with wood and fix just about anything around the house.

Now, at the ripe old age of (almost) 80—and with the effects of creeping dementia clearly showing—he is a mere shadow of his former self. He hasn't ventured downstairs to his workshop in about 10 years. Two years ago, instead of offering a helping hand as I had always come to expect, he only complicated the routine repairing of my own living-room furniture. Sadly, I can't even bring myself to trust him with a saw or a hammer in his hand now.

The dark, winter nights are sometimes the worst. He is somehow convinced that the early nightfall is his cue to wander off to bed—at 7 p.m., in some instances. Making certain that the doors are all locked before calling it a day is another never-ending worry. At times, though, he wakes up at around 10 p.m. to check whether or not the car is still parked in the driveway. Still, it seems the only respite from his many worries is when he sleeps through the night.

This is the hard face of dementia and fading memory—and it leaves a steady trail of reminders. Just the other day I watched him grab a floor mop to sweep a light snow from the back steps. Or I've seen him pour a kettle of unboiled water into the teapot on the stove. I, myself, have forgotten how many times I've witnessed him put things away, only to ask where they've disappeared to five minutes later.

As is often the case with mental illness such as this, routine comes to replace memory recall. He's okay as long as he sticks religiously to his daily regimen. But if he leaves the safe and familiar confines of the house, life becomes a constant worry and sea of confusion.

During the Christmas holidays, for instance, most of the family gathered at my brother's house. I sat next to my father for the entire afternoon. From the moment he sat down, he asked repeatedly about where he had left his shoes, whether his hat was safe on the arm of the chair, and if he was going to be leaving soon. More disturbing was his interminable questioning about when he was next, and whether he had to wait until all the other people seated around him (his own immediate and extended family) had taken their turn.

For some reason, and no one can really know for sure, he thought he was at the doctor's office. He kept saying to me over and over again: "Is it my turn to go into the other room?" Finally, I took him out to my brother's kitchen to see for himself, and, I hoped, to put his mind at ease. All alone in the kitchen, my father turned to me and said with a straight face: "So, how long have you been working here?" Believe me, it's a strange feeling. And I couldn't answer him because I didn't know exactly what to say.

As hard as it is, I have come to accept and live with the realization of being his unrecognizable son. I have come to expect his response when I show up at the house; when he slowly gets up and goes out to the living room and says to Mom: "There's a friend of yours out there." I can't speak for my other brothers and one sister in Vancouver. We don't talk a great deal about these things, preferring instead to remember him as he was; not as he is now.

Naturally, I'm starting to pause and wonder every time I forget a name or mix up my own words when I speak to my students. I find myself thinking that it never used to be this way. But now I'm beginning to think about how long it will be before my own mind starts to go the way of my father's.

Of course, the real hero in all of this is my mother. Not only has she lost a husband and a life-partner, but she has the unenviable task of having to care for him 24 hours a day. It's hard to imagine how difficult, frustrating and stressful this must all be for her. I hate saying it, but she needs to get out of the house more often and take a break from Dad; to have a life for herself outside of what—at least on some days—must seem like a prison. I used to think, when she did take a break, that it was selfish on her part, but now I know that her own mental sanity depends upon it.

Over the years, I have also come to accept my fate and to take comfort from a number of soothing realizations.

Indeed, how many times have I done things only to recall my father having done the exact same things. So, yes, he may not know or remember who I am, but I will most assuredly not forget him. And whenever I contribute to an academic journal or publish something in a newspaper, I oftentimes console myself with the thought that whatever I write contains a piece of my father.

Most of all, it's no longer important that he doesn't recognize who I am. I know who he is, and the person he once was. It makes no difference that I'm a perfect stranger to him. What's important is to spend as much time with him as I can.

So when I stop by now, we just sit and talk, even if it is mostly about the past.

Peter McKenna
Timberlea, N.S.

## MY SON'S LATEST WORD-GAME

As my son and I drive to the Achilles Track Club, at Toronto's Variety Village, he reads billboards, store signs, ads on buses—and anything else he sees in print. Then he asks the meaning of every single word.

"What does 'here' mean? What does 'are' mean? What does '4' mean? What does 'ways' mean?"

The driving is the worst in years. We have been inching along from his house for more than 90 minutes. I am sleep-deprived. His inane questioning is pushing my buttons. Finally, I snap impatiently, "Why are you doing this?"

My adult son, whom some would call autistic, cannot converse well, but he is an expert on word definitions, homonyms, synonyms, antonyms.

These were our tools for language comprehension, reading skills—and his survival.

When he was born, he seemed unfinished. It was as though a control-centre had been lacking. He screamed 24 hours a day and didn't react in instinctual ways to his environment or recognize me as a nurturer. So, I constantly told him what he needed to know, augmenting my words with touch and movement. Early on, I taught him to read.

Since his vision was unreliable and his hearing super-acute, we did lots of word exercises and spelling, and I inundated him with words: he developed a large vocabulary.

This day in the car, I know that he knows the meaning of the words he is asking about. I threaten the silent treatment unless he stops his new-found game. He desists, but conjures up a different version of his game on our return trip. Now he parrots everything I say and goes through the same routine. What does "please" mean? What does "stop" mean? What does "the" mean? What does "nonsense" mean?

I recognize that beneath my anger is fear. Is he regressing? Intuition and experience tell me to play his game for a while. It satisfies him. I am contrite for having been so impatient.

Days later, the rationale for my son's word game hits me with a tornado-like force. I realize he has instinctively been deleting and cleaning up his mental file-folders, doing some neurological organization, in order to achieve useful communication.

There have been many distinct stages in my son's language development.

First there was the song cycle. As a youngster, he constantly listened to the radio, records, and tapes and knew an amazing number of songs. In an attempt to communicate, he selected phrases and sentences from his albums. Sometimes they were apt. Just as often they weren't.

Can you imagine the confusion and frustration of a child who did not understand simple concepts like in, on, up, down, between, front, back, far, near, hard, soft, big, small?

Without a body image (and with a faulty body-mind connection, a mis-wiring), none of these concepts is simple.

To help him acquire understanding of these concepts, we climbed UP the slide and slid DOWN; crawled IN and OUT of tubes, ran BETWEEN the trees and bounced HARD and SOFT balls. Looked FAR and NEAR for BIG and SMALL objects. We always named and verbalized our actions and did many repetitions to help him develop a body image and learn who and what he was in relation to the world.

His next phase, echolalia, was terribly frustrating. Like a trained parrot, he repeated everything he heard. What did he understand? Who knew?

During the latter part of this phase, if you asked him if he wanted an apple or an orange, he could only reply, "Apple."

Doubtless there are substantive, neurological explanations for this phenomenon. But theory seemed totally irrelevant when dealing with an agitated, hyperactive, frustrated child.

Most of the time he talked in what I called a verbal tossed-salad. His articulation, pronunciation and intonation of words was perfect. But the words lacked focus and meaning.

When he was a youngster, we met his sister and a staff member in the hallway of her elementary school. My son, who adored his sister, immediately started jabbering away when he saw her.

The startled staff member asked my daughter what language her brother was speaking. Without missing a beat she replied, "Jonish." A take on his name.

Until very recently, my son used a technique he devised to try to stay connected during conversations. After hearing a statement he would reply with bridging phrases: "And," "Such as," "Like what?" "And then what?" "And after that?"

After years of being stuck, my son's communication has made an unprecedented surge. Why would an adult's language suddenly bloom?

"Mom, I can do things when I am ready."

He is no longer institutionalized and that may have facilitated his readiness. He is again connected to family and community. He has supporters. He belongs to the Achilles Track Club—a group for gutsy achievers with disabilities. He now understands that much of the pain and distancing in his life was due to bureaucracy, not due to family betrayal. So the phrase "I can" is back in his vocabulary. My son, who could get lost walking from one end of the house to the other, will now redirect me in giant parking lots. "No, Mom, it's this way."

His new word-game? It was just transitory. Instead he has treated me to snatches of spontaneous, honest-to-goodness conversation that have flowed so naturally it is hard to believe that this is a mint-new, unfolding skill.

He may yet emerge as the true orator in the family.

*Lucy Mekler*
Toronto, Ont.

# FROM "BABY SOUP" TO "BATHING SUIT"

She fumbles for my ear.

When she finds it, she sets her lips on the outside of my ear breathing heavily into it as she thinks of something to say.

"Ummm," she starts, still waiting for words to arrive. Her hot breath rolls into my ear, filling it with sticky sounds.

"Christmas . . . um . . . birthday party . . . um . . . presents . . . ah . . . grandma . . . candy store, suckers . . . and slides, swimming pool, dessert."

It's my two-year-old daughter, Elise. I sit and listen because I love how her secret feels in my ear, as her little hands dance on the back of my neck.

And I realize that she's giving me a precious gift, a string of her most-prized words, beaded sound, threaded on breath for my ears only.

She's the same one who always asks for me to whisper things into her ears, especially goodnight. My whisper isn't nearly as sticky. It's drier, I think, and the words I use don't burn beats on the eardrum.

She pulls my ear to her mouth again, as she remembers a fragment of another secret she can tell. "Baby soup," she says. I know her words translate to "bathing suit" in a grown-up vocabulary.

Her mouth strings syllables together in a way that no dictionary could track. As she talks, her secrets plant meaning in me. They take me where a dictionary cannot go, to the uncommon sense of what childhood means: childhood sounds like one of Elise's secrets.

Childhood looks like Elise does, after she dresses herself. "I do it myself," she insists as she slams the door to her bedroom. Then after a five-minute storm of huffs and puffs in a fabric fight, she emerges with a turtle-neck shirt, with her lithe, writhing middle somehow squeezed into the neck hole, the bottom of the shirt dangling open around her neckline like a bell. A pair of Teletubbies panties, on backwards with the gusset hugging her left hip. "I did it *myself*," she says proudly.

I wear clothes just as they were supposed to be worn. I find no new way to wear my underwear, nor do I wear my shirt upside down simply because it's possible.

Sometimes Elise sits on my knee and presses her forehead against mine for a quiet chat. In the growing warmth between our bodies, I catch hints of apple juice and chocolate cake. I spy the sheen of apple juice flecked with brown cake crumbs swabbed generously around her mouth, lolling down the cape of her chin.

Forehead to forehead we sit, and I imagine she who smells of apple juice and chocolate cake smells strains of my day—photocopier, cold coffee, book mould.

On her cheeks are tears, ones that have fallen because she has. She pokes one of her small fingers into a tear and holds it out for my tongue.

"Salty," she says. She watches me taste it as if she might see what salty looks like. Then, content with what she sees, she kisses me, and I taste mostly apple juice with a hint of chocolate. Again, I learn. Childhood is the taste of Elise's tear and the smell of a kiss of apple juice and chocolate cake.

Childhood feels like Elise's fresh-bathed skin. I watch her wiggle out of the bath, sink deep into a towel, and come and sit on my knee. I dry her hair. She's so clean, her skin is so young, she feels almost sticky again—sticky clean.

Now, she's fascinated with her belly button. She squeezes it from both sides with her hands. "Closed," she says. She lets go. "Open."

She feels her own skin with some sense of wonder, as though it feels new to her too. "You do it, Dad," she says. I lift my shirt and squeeze my belly button, and she says, "Closed." I let it go and she says, "Open." She squints at my recessed "inny" and looks down at her own again. She runs her finger inside my belly button and wiggles it, feeling the wound that began my childhood so long ago. It's scaled, and filled with lint.

I touch her belly button and she jumps as if the connection is still live. I feel the jolt as I touch her too, and pull away. The lesson is complete. I know what childhood means. She's taken me beyond the dictionary again.

A dictionary is a book of seeds. It contains the dry husks of words that have not yet rooted in living, waiting to find their meaning. The dictionary tells me nothing about how a word lives or finds a home in worlds. But I learn.

The word "childhood" grows up in me suddenly. I feel the senses of the word bud and branch in my brain.

And I tremble.

The word now lives in me.

*Bill Bunn*
Calgary, Alta.

## EVERYBODY NEEDS A MATRIARCHY

I need a matriarchy. This is absolutely true.

A friend of the family recently underwent heart surgery and will spend the next five weeks on the couch—restricted movement—no working and no driving. I've known this man, Juan Carlos, since I was a child. (This was not so long ago; I'm now 25.)

I have visited his relatives in their small village in rural El Salvador. We worked together for more than two years to build a library in that same village, and my experiences as an organizer and as a tourist in Latin America are explicitly informed by my friendship with this man. He is wise, humble and passionate.

One of the only people for whom I have even greater respect is his wife, Claudia. For her accomplishments as an individual, for putting up with an assured, macho man for more than 30 years, and for her friendship—I love this woman. She is my senior by no less than a quarter of a century (I wouldn't consider asking for an exact number) and, from a distance, she is a mother figure to me.

I am fortunate to have many women in my life about whom I can say the same. These include my mother, whose passing almost five years ago has of course removed her from my life, but has not eliminated her presence altogether. She too, from a distance, is still a morally and emotionally tangible figure. This is often clear to me in the simplest of moments.

I find distinct comfort in the company of older women whom I love and respect. Women with whom silence acknowledges age, gender and history while conversation occasionally (or even often) falls short. Ideally family relationships in general can be described in such a way, but for me and, I believe, for many others, these weighty silences, although often comfortable, are sometimes difficult to cherish.

Families are political organisms, they are highly gendered and have the unique ability to always forgive and never forget. They acquire habits and patterns and serve some people better than others. My relationship with my personal matriarchy—my mom and, more recently, relatives and the unrelated women whom I hold dear—has always seemed to subvert the sometimes-problematic family structure.

The time spent, the sentiments shared and the dynamics created seem like clandestine manifestations of some rebellious movement that gathers not for revolt, but simply for togetherness. The most recent meeting of this underground took place for me when I took Claudia shopping one afternoon.

Claudia and Juan Carlos live in the suburbs and she doesn't drive, so I volunteered my Friday afternoon. After making sure than Juan Carlos was well fed, clothed and comfortable, and after thoroughly briefing the homecare worker, we were off.

From the moment we drove out of the parking lot, I was home—or at least in my old neighbourhood, and it had been too long since my last visit. At first I didn't understand why I had been so quickly overtaken by a good mood. I had just spent two hours talking to an old friend about his near-death experience, the whole time mesmerized by the scar revealed by an open shirt on a hot day. In truth this was not a scar, but an only recently closed nine-inch wound.

Why was I pleased-as-punch to be waiting for a price check on men's slippers at Zeller's? I've always found inclusion in the day-to-day life of the matriarch to be calming and, simultaneously, flattering. An hour later I was literally grinning as I carried all of the groceries out of a nearby supermarket while Claudia lugged only her small purse.

Our burdens couldn't have been allotted any other way. *Viva la revolución!* I was smiling because I felt safe. I was smiling because I felt extremely strong and vulnerable, for me an often elusive combination.

I can still remember the difference between running errands with my grandmother and running errands with her and my grandfather together. My grandfather seemed so distracting to this otherwise self-possessed, pro-active woman. She changed so much in his presence, while he conversely seemed to be even more himself when she was in the room.

Perhaps I just love the attention, or perhaps I have been lucky enough to recognize certain rare contexts wherein the power structure is equitable and compassionate. In these contexts, I often miss my mom. In these contexts I have learned that being and becoming a man are indeed the same subjective journey, worthy of contemplation and in need of an always-open mind.

When Claudia called to tell me that Juan Carlos was returning from the hospital, I was putting up decorations for my daughter's third birthday party. Later that same day, I waded through a house full of people and poked my head into my daughter's room. My daughter was with the women closest to her, they were sitting around laughing—it was a beautiful thing. She will know these women for years to come. I gave a quick smile and left the room.

I had never before savoured the taste of rejection. I was so pleased to see my little girl in circumstances that would make her grandmother proud. She was indeed among a matriarchy of her own.

*Arlo Kempf*
Toronto, Ont.

## THE DILEMMA OF A DREAM DOLL LIVING IN OUR HOUSE

The biggest dilemma I have had as a mother is Barbie.

My mother was politically opposed to Barbie. Well, she would never have said it was a political thing: she just said she didn't think that kids should be playing with anything that looked like "that," which I have since interpreted as "a ridiculously overdeveloped hooker-cum-prom-queen."

I was never allowed to have one, so of course I wanted one desperately.

Not that I remember lusting over illicit Barbies, but my mother very clearly does. She remembers me asking for one, over and over.

But as I have gotten older, it has become kind of a point of pride for me: "Oh no, I never had a Barbie."

And then, *sotto voce:* "My mother didn't believe in them."

I do remember going over to a friend's house to play with hers. She had everything Barbie. She had a Barbie makeup case, a Barbie Dream House, all the Barbie accoutrements. Including several Kens. But who cared about Ken, right?

When my daughter was just about to turn three, she sent her first letter to Santa and she only asked for two things in the world: a piggy bank and a Barbie.

My mother was horrified: "You're not going to give her one, are you?"

The agony.

I asked every friend I had ever had about their Barbie experiences. I became obsessed with Barbie and how she had shaped those I knew and their lives.

I compiled a thick file-folder filled with Barbie clippings. I have articles that say that Barbie would be too lean to menstruate, if she really existed. Hell, she probably wouldn't be able to stand up, what with those stiletto-friendly feet.

But eventually I compromised. Remembering how much I wanted Barbie just because she was forbidden fruit in my household, I had to figure out a way to let my daughter have one without implicating myself or trashing my own political ideals.

So, guess what? *Santa* brought Barbie into my daughter's life—I had nothing to do with it. And not really Barbie: Barbie's little sister Skipper, who has a slightly more anatomically correct body (being an adolescent, she hasn't had time to develop a 48D bustline, and her feet are flat instead of at a ski-slope angle).

But then after all the angst and hair-pulling decision-making I had gone through, at my daughter's birthday party two weeks after Christmas, two more Barbies arrived, courtesy of the kids at school.

Full-fledged full-chested Hula-hair Barbie ("the longest hair ever!") and Bubbling Mermaid Barbie, known affectionately in our household as Bubble-head Barbie: when you pour the solution into her crown and squeeze her, bubbles actually emerge from her tiny head.

Oh, we've decapitated a few Barbies since then (complain to Mattel if her head comes off; in our experience, they'll replace her if she's headless within a year of purchase) and we've gained a few extra Barbies (equestrian Barbie, fairy princess Barbie . . .).

We have a Barbie bin under the bed where all the Barbies live in abject misery, I'm sure, tossed in face-down and sealed tightly when not in use.

We have a Barbie motorcycle that a friend presented to us, which makes me laugh because Barbie's skirts are too tight for her to wrap her disproportionate gams around her little pink hog.

After all that, my daughter never really ever played with Barbie: she would get one, put some clothes on it, take them off again and chuck the newest addition into the bin.

She's older now and way over Barbie, and the Barbie bin and its contents are headed for our spring yard sale.

But she never fails to remind me about my knee-jerk reaction to doll-dom's favourite icon.

My daughter makes me laugh. Barbie never hurt her or warped her spirit—she's an ardent 10-year-old feminist and proud to call herself one.

And in the end, we can turn on Scandinavian pop group Aqua's song *Barbie Girl* and dance around our kitchen singing: *"I'm a Barbie girl, in a Barbie world . . ."*

She thinks it is an ode.

I claim it's satire.

*Alison Lawrence*
Toronto, Ont.

## FIELDING QUESTIONS ABOUT LIFE

There had been altogether too much talk about crisis and security and air strikes and danger. We had just returned from a fall visit to England and even four-year-old Sam, innocence personified, had been part of a world that left no one untouched. No dream unmolested, not even his.

"I dreamed about plane crashes in my last sleep," he told me.

The world was too much with us. It was time to get the boots on and head for The Back Field.

A world apart, The Back Field rises from the windy northern quarter of our farm, cresting like a slow rolling wave over the ice-age hill, full and complete in its encircling palisade of oak, maple, white birch and spruce. Early on a good crisp day in October, if I'm lucky, the geese will just skim the hilltop and I can feel and hear the wind vortices of their V-formation just above me as they head south. Maybe a fox will pass; last spring there was a bear.

But today there would be no geese. Just Sam and I, surrounded by the ancient trees and saplings, wind-tossed cloud cover and distant rumblings of winter.

Katy and I had always wanted to give shelter to the childhood realms of our kids. If it was possible to build a storybook world and let them live in it, then good. If free from the tarnishing influence of the 21st century's darker aspects, then better. And this field, at the centre of our old farm, hours away from the city, worlds away from the war zones, was where we directed the little hands and feet for the most quiet peace of all.

So Sam and I walked and talked. He could talk a lot, as four-year-olds often can, and, freed from the dumbfounding sensory overload of Piccadilly Circus and Trafalgar Square, he was able to air out his mind and go off on a rich variety of tangents: Bob the builder. When's my birthday? I am Robin Hood, watch me shoot my bow and arrow. What am I getting for christmas? Daddy, are you a hero?

I didn't much like that last one. To him, I hoped I was a hero, but he was getting around to something deeper and more troublesome. He'd heard the television news in passing, seen the coloured photos in The Times, heard discussions on the Underground, seen the soldiers at the fenced-off entry to Downing Street.

A walk in The Back Field had to be an antidote, however gradual. Farmer Ron Hewitt had ploughed while we were away and the soil smelled rich and full of promise. Next August, this field would be a sea of his special strain of sweet corn.

"Raccoons love corn, Sam. Let's talk about raccoons."

I thought of my own Dad, working these fields during the Second World War, struggling to keep the John Deere together, picking a fresh crop of rocks every spring, looking at adolescent versions of the same trees that now towered along the western horizon. If anybody had been in the safe central haven of peace in 1940, it had been him, broadcasting wheat seeds by hand, back here in The Back Field.

But the de Havilland Aircraft Co., builder of the Mosquito bomber, got some of its parts from a local factory in Orillia, Ont., and from time to time would send a bomber for a fly-past, rattling farmhouse windows and bringing a deep rumbling of patriotic pride to the workers below. It was a visceral tie to the war effort, a sudden deafening reminder that the world's problems were a lot closer than you might think. We're all in it together, lads—that sort of thing.

For my Dad, spreading seed in a quiet corner of Ontario in 1940, it was a jarring reality check. A reminder that no man is an island.

But that was a different time and a different war, and Sam and I enjoyed our peace, unruffled by the throaty roar of a twin-engined bomber. Somewhere off to the south, we could hear a dump truck shift down for a hill, but that was it. Snow clouds were massing out over Georgian Bay but, for now, peace reigned.

Can we ever really give our children the nurturing isolation we think they need? Can we hope to preserve their innocence? We try, but are we kidding ourselves? Do the words "terrorist" and "anthrax" and "cluster-bomb" need to be part of their vocabulary?

We change the subject when the uncomfortable gets too uncomfortably close. "Let's talk about raccoons, Sam," I say, but I really want to say, "Sam, I wish your injured world was different, my little one."

He asks if I'm a hero, but I think he's really saying: "Daddy, will you keep me safe?"

Safe? How could he not be safe back here, in the quiet centre of solitude?

And then, as if cued by God for maximum effect, a massive airliner, maybe a 747, thunders by overhead, climbing from Toronto, headed for Europe. Full of people. Full of fuel. The mind's projector wants to replay the horrible images again: the planes swinging around and lining up the towers . . .

Sam sees the plane too, and to him, it is right over us, its shadow ready to collide with ours. What plays on the little screen in his mind?

I want to stick out my chest like Rat in *The Wind in the Willows* and say, "Beyond the Wild Wood comes the Wide World, and that's something that doesn't matter, either to you or me. . . . Don't ever refer to it again, please."

But I can't. It's as clear as the vapour trail that veers sharply off to the east above us.

The Wide World is right here, Sam. And yes, little one, we are all in this together.

He takes my hand. For now, that seems good enough for him.

*David Gillett*
Orillia, Ont.

## THE REMOVAL OF MY FAVOURITE BREAST

"This is a plain fibro adenoma. This can't turn cancerous any more than any other part of your body." A fine needle biopsy had proven this hazelnut-sized lump to be benign and I relaxed. Now, as I look at the long slash crossing out where my left breast used to be, I recall those comforting words of the specialist, reassuring me that I didn't need to have this little lump removed.

A year after being reassured, during my routine physical exam, my doctor feels apprehensive about the same lump and sends me back into the program. Though the lump is slightly larger and flatter, I am told it is typical of a fibro adenoma. No other tests are recommended and again I am booked for a follow-up appointment. In the meantime, I have a moment of enlightenment inspired by my dog, Cleo. The growing lumps that she has on her back are fat deposits, which, if not removed when they are small, end up involving a bigger incision and a drainage tube. Thinking about my small breast and the palpable lump I make a practical decision to have it removed.

A few weeks later I sit on the examination table as three strangers enter the room, one being the surgeon who is on shift for the day. I look at him hopefully, as he is about to give me the expected biopsy results from the lumpectomy.

"Unfortunately, this has turned out to be cancer. The good news is that it is grade one but you'll have to have more surgery. We have an appointment booked immediately for you to see your family doctor." His stone face moves in speech as my face deepens in colour, my head slowly tilting downwards. Within seconds they depart leaving me alone with my verdict, which feels like a conviction of some sort. They never even bother to see how well my wound is healing. My war against cancer begins that day as I drive home alone in a daze, lost in myriad confusing thoughts.

At night I lie against my husband, his chest hair wet with my tears, as his hand covers my small left breast. It is my favourite one. It fits perfectly into the palm of his hand. He caresses it gently as I recall the stinging sensation of milk rushing in when one of my babies would latch on hungrily. I thank this breast for its sensuality and for its nourishment.

Not long after, I leave the hospital and a week later a nurse pulls out drainage tubes from under my arm. A week after that, I am unstapled, feeling no sensation as she presses and pulls on my skin.

"You're healing well. You're looking good," she says brightly. I smile at her, grateful for her tender care of me. Looking down I see a flat surface with red track marks running across it like a railway line. A train of sadness passes through me. My eyes dampen momentarily. My left breast, small and precious, is gone.

The oncologist tells me that because they found cancer in two of my lymph nodes, my chemotherapy will increase from four to six months. My head drops as I try to absorb the words, realizing that had action been taken two years ago, it may not have spread this far. She speaks positively about aiming for a total cure. The unknown looms larger, drawing me into its void as I struggle to listen to medical diagnosis and advice. My thoughts are distracted and I'm thinking about God. Do I really believe in a Divine plan?

Does God exist? Everyone's days are numbered but suddenly my name is called to have my timetable discussed. I desperately want to skip out.

"Aren't you mad, Mom?" My 16-year-old son asks as we drive home from his work.

"At what?" I ask.

"Well, you're my mom. By not telling you that there was a chance of this becoming cancer, they were basically committing attempted murder." I appreciate the intensity in his large, brown eyes. A long discussion follows that prompts me to think beyond myself to other women in the same situation. I would like to see change. How to help bring about more responsibility, diligence and accountability is edging in on my thoughts. Five weeks later, on Mother's Day, my son carefully shaves my head, leaving me with a Mohawk first and then just a tuft of hair at the back of my head. I could pretend to be a Buddhist monk.

"Aren't you mad, Rita?" My sister chokes on words through sobs after first hearing my diagnosis.

"Mad, at what?" I ask.

"Mad . . . at that word . . . CANCER!" She spills her thoughts and is released from the strangling power of the word. The tears follow. Before my surgery she has a day of mourning for my breast. For me, every day embodies some grief. Anger hasn't occurred to me yet. I relate to shock and sadness. Sometimes a dark, foreboding cloud begins to descend upon me. Its suffocating weight presses down, reminding me of past years of debilitating depression. I go and sit in my favourite spot in the living room, put on soothing music and saturate myself with inspiring words that have brought healing to me in the past year.

Merton, Sister Faustina, Nouwen, Fenelon, Sanford, St. Francis de Sales and King David have mentored me and directed my thoughts to my inner resources. I have a physical illness that needs treatment but my soul rests secure. The dark cloud dissipates, fear and anxiety vanish: I am weightless once again.

I walk into the place where I volunteer, visiting with HIV and AIDS patients, feeling more one with them with my nausea, fatigue and physical changes. Another volunteer, in his 60s, who vacillates in happiness according to how well his sex life is going, caringly asks me about my illness and whether I am considering reconstructive surgery. I tell him no. "Besides, I am content and it doesn't matter anyway," I say. With a serious glance he drops words like bricks: "Believe me, it matters!"

A judgment of undesirability and damaged goods assails me. I remind myself that he is a restless man who perhaps still doesn't know the meaning of the words "intimacy" and "love."

My counsellor/friend knows me and will not allow me to become detached but keeps me closely connected with my body. I must treasure, respect and care for it. It is the imperfect home in which my soul resides and where my creative self exuberantly shouts, "I am!"

Look deeply into my blue eyes and you will see the soul of a beautiful woman dancing free. I will never be disfigured. I have lost my breast but I haven't lost me.

*Rita Janet Dhahan*
Vancouver, B.C.

## CINNAMON BITS AND STUPID SHEEP

Years ago, as my two-year-old and I were walking out of the General Store on Bowen Island, B.C., someone said, "Fuck."

Minutes later, snug in his car seat, Jesse was chanting the word, over and over. During the day, it continued to burst forth, like surprise popcorn kernels that sail out of the pot.

How was it possible that a bombardment of parental "pleases" and "thank yous" had such a modest effect, while one curse from a stranger had such impact?

Jesse, at four said, "Damn it" as he was struggling to fit two pieces of Duplo together. Naturally, he was playing with my mother-in-law, who raised her eyebrows in my direction.

"His father taught him," I said, adding a little too quickly, "At least he used it in context."

Jesse had forgotten the F-word after a week or so of no one using it (within earshot), but was reacquainted with it in Grade 2. The classroom bully, who was pestering Jesse, got caught. In his defence, he blurted, "Jesse said the F-word!"

Both boys were taken to the principal's office.

"Did you say the F-word?" asked the principal.

"No," said Jesse.

He was believed and dismissed.

When Jesse related the story to me that evening, his big brown eyes met mine as he asked, "What is the F-word?"

After a brief hesitation and finding no easy way out, I told Jesse the F-word, its meaning and why it mustn't ever be used. He couldn't understand why the word was "bad," and even recalled inadvertently making rhymes with it in the past. Nonetheless, he promised never to use it, and never to tell it to his younger brother, Elliot.

But as promises go, this one was hard to keep and Jesse regularly suggested that Elliot was old enough to know about the F-word. So one day, as we were driving to Jesse's piano lesson, he suddenly announced, "I think it's time that Elliot knew the F-word."

"What's the F-word?" asked Elliot, five years old at that time.

I panicked. "No, Jesse!" I said. "Just drop it."

Elliot persisted and started revving up into a tantrum over the secrecy of the F-word.

"Is it idiot?" he asked, remembering that we'd recently spoken about this word.

"Is it stupid?" he tried, getting more desperate, kicking his feet on the front seat.

And then I panicked. Again. "Yes."

Elliot clapped his hands together. "Stupid! Stupid! Stupid!" he shrieked gleefully.

I reasoned with myself that at least s and f sounded similar over the telephone.

But everything backfired when we went to fetch Jesse from his lesson half an hour later.

The piano teacher had sheep in a paddock beside her house. During several conversations about animal intelligence in the past, sheep rated low. Upon spotting them grazing naively upon the grass, Elliot burst from the car, overjoyed at the opportunity to make use of his restricted word. He rushed to the fence rails, dancing about and singing, "F-word sheep! F-word sheep! F-word sheep!"

I was thankful not to have my mother-in-law along.

This brings me to cinnamon bits. Jesse, now nine, has an eclectic taste in music and particularly favours fiddle. Jesse's dad Peter burned a CD for him with an assortment of music including *The Devil Went Down to Georgia* by the Charlie Daniels Band. In it are the words "son of a bitch," and when Peter played it on the stereo while the kids danced around the house, he turned down the volume at the swearing part.

Perhaps Peter figured the kids would never want to listen to this song without a supervisor poised on the volume dial. Of course, this didn't make me feel like such a ninny for the

"F-word sheep" incident. At least our parenting styles are somewhat consistent. Eventually, Jesse listened to the tune in its entirety with a friend, and was hastily informed that "son of a bitch" was swearing.

Wow! That was a sweet discovery and one to share with Elliot!

So Jesse played the tape for Elliot and paused at the best bit.

"No Jesse!" I snapped, giving him "the look."

He realized his mistake immediately, but it was too late.

"What did it say?" yelled Elliot. "Tell me what it said!"

"Let's move on to The Bare Naked Ladies," I tried.

Elliot was gearing up for some major vocals, when he suddenly sucked in his lips, narrowed his eyes and inquired, "Was it cinnamon bits?"

"Yes!" Jesse shouted, a chip off the ol' block. "It's cinnamon bits!"

"Cinnamon bits! Cinnamon bits! Cinnamon bits!" Elliot shouted gleefully, his fists punching the air above his head.

I tried to give him a stern look. "Now you know what it is, but you mustn't say it any more."

He said it about 50 more times, then asked, "What does it mean?"

I needed to say something fast before Jesse answered. "Someone who's not very bright," I said, inwardly chastising myself for not being more creative. After all, we already had the F-word.

That evening as I tucked Jesse into bed, he whispered, "If Elliot believes that story, then he's really cinnamon bits!"

This, I figure, is how families distinguish themselves from each other.

*Valerie Rolfe Lupini*
Victoria, B.C.

# FRIENDS

## COOKING THINGS UP IS FOR THE BIRDS

Almost every morning, I have coffee at Diane's house. She is not afraid to use 18 per cent cream and slips a spoonful of sugar into my coffee whenever she thinks I might need it. I suspect it is on those particular days when unwinding my joints and muscles takes more time than usual and I need some soothing help. Or it could be just a certain look she sees on my face. She is generally right about whatever it is she sees. I know that because the sugar always comes at exactly the right time. Then the coffee is transformed into a statement about our friendship. Warm, comfortable, knowing and forgiving.

Starting my day this way has become a ritual. Sipping light-creamed coffee and sharing space with Diane. We sit in our usual chairs in front of the big window and watch the fluffy winter sparrows fighting for space on two feeders. The squirrels are there, too, and hug the feeders upside down with their noses in the trough. I laugh to myself when I hear her trying to take a stern tone with them.

The winter before last, before she started to feed the birds, Diane fed the neighbourhood. Her Mom, her friends, her kids' friends. And you didn't necessarily have to be there to eat. A plate would appear at the house. The food was flying. At that time, I was especially grateful since my relationship with cooking was at an all-time low. In the words of a hungry friend who came to my house during that period to find only a coconut in the fridge, "How do you get away with it?"

I have Diane, I replied.

Then something happened. One morning, I walked up Diane's snowy driveway and heard a sound like a portent of some disturbing emotional cloud inside the house that the birds were picking up on. They were making a noise right out of Alfred Hitchcock's movie *The Birds*. It sounded as though every bird in the locality had come to sit in Diane's bushes. A little worried, I pulled my coat closer and hurried up to the door with unusual haste and found Diane in the kitchen looking pensive. I mentioned the noise I had heard on the way in. She had noticed it too. "I've made up my mind," she said. "I'm not going to feed those birds anymore."

I was a little skeptical upon hearing this, but I grabbed my coffee and sat down to listen to the sad news while eyeing the sparrows, who were flicking most of the seed to the ground. Soon the pigeons, who had also come to Diane's yard, would rise up in a cloud to mingle with the scattering sparrows and the vigilant squirrels, as dog Oscar made his first manoeuvre of the morning by dashing out the back door. Although a large dog, he looked a bit like a mutant bird standing there on the snow pile with his head at the level of the bird feeders.

"Pigeons are really just birds too," I ventured. Ever generous, Diane agreed that, yes, pigeons are birds but with a flinty look in her eye that I had seen when we spoke of starlings: She stood her ground and maintained that she didn't like them anyway.

"I don't cook anymore," Diane said in a tone that was searching for an answer to this mystery. I didn't ask her what that had to do with birds. Diane and I are much like the Odd Couple. Modified forms of Oscar and Felix. For a moment, I was afraid that some of my bad habits had rubbed off on her.

On reflection, I decided that there are more similarities. We are both searching for the same things except that she is a lot neater while she searches. I have not really cooked for a long time and I had come to think of Diane as a permanent rock in the stream of culinary art. I felt I had serious cause to worry about her, since my own disconnection from food came out of a disconnection with the universe in general. (It hasn't turned out to be quite that serious.)

Over time, over coffee, we have decided a few things about cooking. Mainly, there have probably been just too many birds at our bird feeders and for too long. We have both developed a real fondness for microwave reheating, sandwiches, eggs and anything that can be made in a large pot, although that can be tricky. As my daughter said to me when she asked me to make lunch one day, "Just don't make anything disgusting."

We have decided that cooking is, for both of us, a monitor of our relationship with the world. We always share stories of the rare times when food preparation happens to turn into an offering and we feel our internal pilot lights flare briefly. It gives us hope that there is cooking in our futures.

In the meantime, we scan *Oprah* and the bookstores for insight. Diane gave me her copy of *The Course in Miracles* and I tell her about my psychotherapy. It doesn't sound like much of an exchange for Diane, but in a strange and pleasant way it works.

We are quite different. It used to be that Diane would toss out food she felt was in poor condition. I used to bring her stale donuts because they were a bargain. We are moving towards some mutual point. She eats leftovers now and I stay away from the squishy banana sale.

I figure that when our lines of movement intersect someday it will be another Phenomenon. In our enlightened state we'll end up on *Oprah,* of course, with our new philosophy of life which will be something like, "Just keep moving, eventually you'll get somewhere."

Diane is still feeding the birds.

*Jane Dunn*
Ottawa, Ont.

## WEEDING THE FRIENDSHIP GARDEN

Perhaps you've glanced at recently published lists in fashion magazines advising us sheep, without taste or brains, what's "in" for the coming year.

These non-negotiable, bulleted lists itemize fashionable skirt lengths, popular bar drinks, evocative fragrances and prevailing attitudes toward sex, health and heels.

None of the lists I've seen, however, focuses on current fads in friendships. This is because in 2001, like every preceding year, low-pressure, high-quality, mood-enhancing friendships are "in."

Eternally "in" friendships generally describe people who enjoy spending time together and who contribute a fairly proportionate amount of energy, intellect and dollars to the friendship. These relationships grow out of demonstrated actions of trust, respect and loyalty and foster honest communication about difficult issues.

Perhaps most importantly, these friendships offer exchanges of insightful, open-minded opinion without debilitating judgment.

These most-worthy friends don't pressure you to see them or to call them more often. They simply understand that sometimes you retreat into a low-profile mode or just haven't been able to get to them. Consequently, if you haven't spoken in weeks, or even in months, you could easily pick up where you last left off.

And contrary to popular thought, longevity isn't the most important ingredient of friendship. What you share today is so much more important than trying to revitalize a rusty connection by rehashing juvenile events from some golden time you can both barely remember. I also believe in incredible-friends-at-first-sight. Although I'm certain we meet old souls from other lifetimes, sometimes it's incredibly refreshing to meet someone new with unusual passion, a new perspective—an electric, eclectic meeting that inspires immediate familiarity, understanding or raucous laughter.

It seems that friendships were far easier to maintain during school. We would all invariably wind up at the same bar on Thursday nights and our stresses were largely social; concerns that were inconveniently interrupted by exams, surprise parental visits and overdue papers. Most of us cared less about cultivating karma than locating our next Carlsberg. It was an unreal environment because, for the next few months or years, our lives were clearly mapped out for us. In this homogenous, womb-like existence we only knew that we had to (eventually) pick a major and find a job. Our daily schedule was dictated by how many courses we were taking (minus the ones dropped along the way) and, for the first time, we were referred to as adults, yet we didn't have to contemplate things such as life purpose or life insurance.

Somehow, along the way, many friendships sort of fell away from us, moving beyond the concentric rings of our personal planets. Some fizzled because of geography and others due to stultifying marriages, pukey kids, undivided attention to addictions and the unbearable egos of born-again investment bankers.

Although the cheerleader in me would love to imagine the world as a giant square dance in which we all laugh and spin each other around as we do-si-do, I know this is not reality. Some friendships simply fade away. But it's not as though they are no longer considered friends. It's just that the friendship has become a bit like a dormant bank account. It will continue to store select but salient memories that will be withdrawn and reflected upon from time to time. And, although the account hasn't been fortified with recent deposits, it won't be closed and could be quickly re-activated.

Some friendships, however, have to be actively and permanently weeded. As more of us seek self-preservation, we're not only more aware of how we feel about ourselves, but how we're affected by the company we keep. The bottom line? High maintenance, negative and nasty relationships have to go.

If you're not sure if a friendship should be weeded from your world, there are a few easy tests: First of all, take careful note of how you feel just before you see the friend and immediately afterwards. (Note: exclude anyone who has been recently dumped, fired or driving in downtown

Toronto). Did you arrive or leave feeling insecure, ugly, anxious, aggravated or itchy from a sudden rash? After a visit or phone call from this friend, did you feel elated or crusty? Do you usually look forward to calling them or feel that you have to and will get flogged if you don't? Next, take some time to consider your overall sense of harmony and well-being when you're with them. And, like any rigorous post-date analysis with a love interest, always consider how you feel about the person ex-alcohol.

But before going on a weeding rampage, focus only on the particularly draining, destructive friendships. And keep in mind that each friendship can't be everything and that we're all imperfect and in pain in some way.

Even if a friendship seems limited at times, it may have a unique, very necessary place. For example, I have friends who keep me grounded and open-minded, others for unconditional love over lattes and some simply for sharing a boozy night out with an incident or two. It is the sum of their precious parts that keeps me whole.

For others, I've accepted that a regular weeding of my friendships garden is a tough but necessary exercise—a vigorous extraction of the toxins who consistently choke my spirit. In the long run, it makes my atypical, asymmetrical rows of friendships stronger and more fruitful. It also affords me more energy to luxuriously toil in my friendship garden and frolic to cheap dance tunes like a joyful child among my patches of precious pals. Our tears of laughter and sorrow irrigate our souls, and there, I can protect them from disease or disaster that may try to ravage them.

*Meghan Stothers*
Saltspring Island, B.C.

## WHAT ARE FRIENDS FOR?

I dumped a friend last year. Or maybe she dumped me. It was she who suggested we end our decade-long habit of Sunday morning walks and talks. I readily agreed, though, and felt light-headed with relief. I had slowly come to understand that we weren't friends anymore. Or, maybe we never had been.

This is a friend who goes back to the 1950s. We grew up together in the same town. We had pajama parties and double-dates together. We shared an apartment when we were at university, before our lives took different directions. When we reconnected 10 years ago, after careers, kids, marriages and divorces had taken their toll, it was because we found ourselves living in the same city. It was lovely finding someone nearby with whom I shared a common background and many mutual friends. During most of the nineties, we took time on Sunday mornings to walk in nearby parks, taking the air and setting the world to rights.

At first, I believed that our conversations were eclectic, interesting and stimulating for both of us. My friend and I agreed on absolutely nothing. We were at opposite ends of the spectrum on every topic under the sun. Feminism, sports, taxes, healthcare, education, raising kids, religion— you name it, we disagreed. Even our tastes in clothing, food and architecture put us at odds. We had very different views on how best to manage society, and politics quickly became a flashpoint.

In the early nineties, when the new government got elected in British Columbia, my friend rejoiced, taking pleasure in recounting the scandals of the previous government. No detail was overlooked. The new government, it seemed, let her sleep better. A few years later, after the universe had unfolded a bit, I asked her how she was sleeping, given the endless litany of new government scandals. I wanted to rant too, but she swiftly cut me off, telling me that she didn't want to talk about it. She said that she didn't watch the news anymore. It was too upsetting. I felt cheated, but I knew that I was not totally innocent. We were both strong-minded, stubborn and argumentative.

More and more of our discussions ended with her telling me that we couldn't talk about a topic anymore, if we were to continue our friendship. When, a couple of years ago, she insisted that a condition of our continued walks together would be to observe a lengthy list of taboo subjects, I meekly agreed. I hate rules like that, but my thinking was that at least we would get in a good walk and, after all, it was only a couple of hours and we could talk about our personal lives.

So we continued under her rules. There was no lack of things to talk about. Each of us had experienced both the wonderful and also terrible life events that fate had tossed our way—weddings, births, grandchildren, illnesses and deaths. But no matter what the topic, she made short work of anything I brought up, before turning the talk back to events in her life. Again I felt cheated, but I didn't really mind, because while talk is therapy, so is listening. Besides, it always seemed that her problems were bigger than mine.

For example, when she lost her job of 22 years, not an easy thing when you are closer to 60 than 50, I supported her and commiserated with her. When her 80-something mother died, I went to the funeral, hugged her and helped her clean out her mother's townhouse. When her grand-child was born with a severe birth defect, I cried with her and listened to the weekly reports of hospitalizations, medications and the complete trauma that was inflicted on her family.

When I lost *my* job after 34 years, she observed that I was lucky and that my former employer was far too generous. When my mother died, she asked if my mom smoked, adding that her parents had died of old age. When I told her that my daughter and daughter-in-law had melanoma, she said they must have lain in the sun.

When, last spring, I mentioned a problem mammogram, she said she didn't want to talk about breast cancer. I asked, "Is it because you are afraid that you might get it?" and she nodded unhappily. My friend is afraid that she might not die of old age like her parents.

These were not the reasons why we stopped talking. But one day last spring, when I was agonizing about someone dear to me, whose behaviour had become increasingly erratic, and who I suspected had a serious mental disorder, she said that it was probably my fault. I thought: Friends don't do that to their friends—even if they might be right.

By the time I was diagnosed with breast cancer, we had stopped having our walks. We had nothing to say to each other. To her credit, she called as soon as she heard of my illness. My husband was short with her though, and didn't pass over the phone. We were both stressed at that moment. I felt bad, but I didn't grab the phone away from him. I didn't need to hear her say that it was probably the estrogen therapy that I had been taking that caused it. Later, a mutual friend laughed and told me that the first words out of her mouth were that it was likely the hormone-replacement therapy that had caused my illness. I felt cruel for not speaking to her.

Now I just feel sad. Maybe I should give her a call, ask how she's doing, ask about her kids. But right now I need friends who don't make rules about what we can talk about and who don't pass judgments about who or what caused which of life's misfortunes.

Maybe not enough time has passed for us to resume our relationship.

For now, we agree not to agree in silence.

*Marilyn Baker*
Richmond, B.C.

## ARE GOODY BAGS A GOOD THING?

First they get a star just for going No. 2 in the toilet.

Then there's the goody bag thing. Forgive me if I sound like your cranky grandmother for a moment but, in my day, you went to a birthday party, handed the birthday boy or girl their gift, ate a piece of cake usually made from a box mix, played a round of pin the tail on the donkey, and went on your merry way, lucky if the kid's mother handed you a limp balloon on your way out the door. (Which you then happily tied on your wrist and refused to take off, even in the bathtub, until it met its end when your evil little brother snuck up and popped it with a thumbtack.)

Well those days have gone the way of the rotary telephone.

In today's world, along with the birthday cake purchased at the Belgian *patisserie*, the hired magicians and clowns, pool parties catered by McDonald's, Bonkers, and Chuck E.

Cheese franchises—which if Dante were alive today he'd surely have included in an inner ring of hell—the little party guests have to get something, too. And I'm not talkin' a candy necklace and a few sticks of gum in a brown paper lunch sack decorated with glitter. (I learned my lesson with that one. "That's all?" one sniffling child actually had the gall to inquire, after I handed him a bag miserably deficient in loot.)

There's actually an industry devoted to the bags themselves (Pokémon, Digimon, Hello Kitty, Sailor Moon, *Jurassic Park, 101 Dalmations,* etc.), not to mention what goes inside them: stickers, tattoos, Silly Putty, Bubbles, gel pens, superballs, lollipops with batteries in the stick to make them spin, disposable cameras. It's not difficult to drop $20 per guest; my kids have received goody bags the contents of which were worth more than the price of the gift they brought. One friend's son went to a party where every kid got a remote-controlled car from Radio Shack. Another told me of a party her daughter attended where the girls all got gift certificates for makeovers at Merle Norman. I'm waiting for the day they hand out passes to Disneyworld.

Whatever happened to the concept of the birthday being a special day—special being the operative word—for the person who was *born on that day?* People came to the party to fete you. You, in turn, feted them on their birthday. No, now everything is *me too, me too.* God forbid that someone should feel left out, dejected that another is getting slightly more attention than they are or that a six-year-old might have to learn an iota of self-control: "It's not your turn, Brittany."

This same concept is behind the idea that one should get a trophy at the end of six weeks of soccer just for showing up at least once for practice. I have two boys, and 3,000 trophies in our basement. And my kids are both still in grade school. Someday I will rent a small U-Haul, back it up to the basement door, load it up and drive said trophies to the outskirts of town, where they will join the 400 billion others at the trophy landfill, sharing space with *Most Improved Three-Year-Old* and *Best Left-Handed First Baseman Born in February*.

These children then grow up, and demand recognition just for getting up in the morning—forget about making the bed.

What started my wool-gathering on this topic was the relentless media coverage of the annual award season we are currently in the midst of. Emmys, Tonys, Oscars, Genies, Obies, Grammys, Junos, Golden Globes, SAGS, GLADS, the People's Choice Awards, the TV Guide Awards, blah, blah, blah. The entertainment industry gave out 3,182 awards last year, according to *Los Angeles Magazine*. My favourite hands-down was the Teen Choice Awards' *Best Hissy Fit in a Movie*—for which the winner received a surfboard. Wasn't getting paid to throw a tantrum—something that couldn't have required a great stretch of thespian ability, given that the actor, and I use the term loosely, surely had lots of practice throwing fits throughout childhood, especially when they didn't like the goody bag they got—enough? Where will it end?

But, more importantly, which child psychologist is responsible for the theory that prizes for all promotes good self-esteem? Isn't self-esteem acquired when you actually *earn* something? I imagine the young psychologist, still in graduate school, reading in a biography of Hitler the conjecture that the germ of the Fuhrer's hatred of the Jews was planted when the painting he entered in an art contest didn't win a prize. (The judge was Jewish.) Light bulb goes off in young psychologist's head: "Give 'em all a prize or we might create a monster!" Young psychologist writes bestseller, *Everybody Wins! Developing and Protecting Your Child's Fragile Ego* and is now a consultant to the entertainment industry.

I want that psychologist's head on a platter. Or, alternatively, I want him sentenced to 24 hours community service at Bonkers, to be served consecutively, with only two potty breaks and no Advil.

*Rita Sirignano*
Calgary, Alta.

## THE MYSTERY OF A LOSS DISCOVERED

This winter I laid a ghost to rest. His name was Magnus Magnusson and 35 years ago, he was my friend. Then he vanished from my life and I always wondered what became of him. In December, I went back to my old hometown and now I know.

Magnus first showed up well into our last year of high school and I must have sympathized with him for appearing late in such a crucial year—although I really don't remember, because no one felt sorry for him for long. Magnus was tall and handsome and full of goodwill and openness that made him everyone's favourite.

I had known my other friends since elementary school and it was difficult to think of them in any other way—they were just boys like me. Magnus was different and his nature telegraphed tremendous appeal. When Magnus was around, the girls beamed inexplicably, boys fell uncharacteristically quiet and little kids stuck to him like iron filings to a magnet. For all his height and size, no one could get enough of him. Years later, I decided Magnus was reconciled to his place in the cosmos and that made him seem poised and serene.

Our friendship developed around the fact that we owned motorcycles. While our machines were dissimilar—I had a cool new Honda and Magnus had a moped—they gave us something in common besides school. The fact that he had to pedal his neanderthalic DKW before it came to life never troubled him. Nothing diminished his gratitude for the wretched thing. The Magnussons were farmers and his father had given Magnus the moped so that he could forgo the school bus. As the eldest child, it was important that Magnus do well in high school and also gain a social life. Their farm lay deep in the countryside, so it was like presenting Magnus with wings.

I met Mr. Magnusson only once. In those days, the town had no weekend shopping and the whole place shut down at 5 p.m., except Friday night when stores stayed open until 9 p.m. It was an important community event and everyone looked forward to promenading on main street and to meeting friends. This was especially true for farmers. They rolled into town in big, glittering cars and stepped out wearing their Friday best.

So it was that I bumped into the Magnussons. Mr. Magnusson seemed to know all about me and shook my hand, all the while crowded by Magnus's three young sisters, who skipped among us or dangled from their brother's limbs. It was easy to see they all adored Magnus. Years later, I came to understand that Magnus was the product of unconditional love, a quality at that time unknown to many of his friends.

When school ended, a group of us found summer jobs harvesting peas for a local cannery. Our role was to scamper about in the back of a moving truck and distribute pea vines as they streamed off a harvester. We worked seven days a week, often late into the night.

One day, Magnus surprised us by joining the crew. Life had proved lonely for him once school ended and he convinced his father to let him work at the cannery. For a country kid like Magnus, it was unusual. He came to town on his moped just to board a truck and go harvest someone else's crops. He wasn't with us for long.

Occasionally, a breakdown in the factory caused serious interruptions and on one warm, moonless night, everything stopped. With no trucks to fill, we loader boys had time on our hands. We made billy tea over a fire and found a comfortable grassy ditch where we settled on our backs to talk and identify stars.

Someone spotted a curiously intense glow in the west and Magnus was on his feet in a heartbeat. Before anyone could speak, a piercing light swept the field. A soundless shape as big as a bus plunged across a stand of pines at treetop level, shot over our heads and disappeared.

We scrambled out of the ditch, jabbering our astonishment. Only Magnus seemed to understand and yet he said nothing. He stared toward the east, his face blurred by forces other than the cover of night. It was as though he had once experienced something similar and it terrified him.

Soon, the trucks returned and we went back to work. We parted at the cannery gate in the early hours of the morning and later heard that Magnus had quit. At the end of the summer, we chose our career paths, went our separate ways and heard no more of Magnus.

This past December, I returned home for the first time in 17 years and set about finding old friends. Magnus had been on my mind for years and, anyway, I longed to discuss the incident in the pea fields.

Now, a great deal can happen in 35 years and I was prepared for anything—or so I thought. Magnus, I discovered, had been dead all that time. He had died soon after I left town and the news never caught up to me. He had been riding home on his moped late one night and was killed in a head-on collision with a speeding car.

It seemed strange to feel shock and grief for a boy who died 35 years ago, yet my emotions skittered and rolled as though I had seen him the week before. I just couldn't believe he was dead. All that time, I imagined him happily occupying a space somewhere on the planet and I had only to find it. The space, it turned out, was a cemetery plot.

Later, I found comfort in the notion that Magnus had not been dead but existed in the everlasting youth that is memory. Had I known of his death in 1966, I may have forgotten him by now. Instead, his grace and innocence remain as fresh and real as on the day we met.

His death also obliges me to examine my own circumstances. In experiencing the trials and disappointments of middle age, it is helpful for me to remember that Magnus tasted none of them. For me, life, thus far, is good. For him, it wasn't "a waste," as is said about the loss of a young life. For Magnus, it was no life at all.

Of the flight over the pea fields, I offer no more expla-
nation than anything about Magnus. It was a phenomenon
that shrinks to insignificance when I search his death for
meaning. His loss remains the greater mystery.

> *Colin Haskin*
> Toronto, Ont.

## KICK THIS, PROFESSOR POINDEXTER

It's called prof ball and it is an attempt to reinvent soccer so
that profs—aging and not, male and not, competitive and
not—can work off what we in the profession call "scholar's
ass." Prof ballers aspire to a gentler, more cooperative
way than is typical of life in the ivory tower. Not long
ago, Will, the wonderfully congenial prof ball organizer
for our campus, had to issue an edict: "We need to ban
hard shots. In the indoor game, shots are taken from very
close range and few of us have the reflexes to stop a good
hard shot, much less protect our person. Let's agree to
limit shots to around 50-75 per cent of full force. That
way, nobody gets hurt.

"Goals scored via hard shots will henceforth not count
and will be greeted with cries of 'No good, too hard!' from
the defending team. Errant hard shots will be greeted with

cries of 'Shame!' and the expectation of full repentance by the offending player."

Since it was my "person" (or "manhood" as they say on the street), that had been pounded flat, eliciting this new rule, and since I am presently on sabbatical writing a book on performance—ritualistic, theatrical and athletic—I laid claim to the right to wax philosophical.

Not long after, while I was still limping and after my toenail fell off, my wife, Susan, asked, "So, how much more are you willing to sacrifice for prof ball?"

"Sacrifice?" I said. "It's not just us religious studies types who use this kind of terminology, so do the cultural historians. They say that the history of athletics is replete with ritual that is essentially sacrificial."

Wife of many years, she grinned. She's used to cowboy-academic hyperbole.

Then on Tuesday, as we were warming up for indoor soccer, I counted five people pounding the ball into the walls, basketball goals and nets.

Repeatedly. Ritually. Usually there were one or two. Now five.

I remember saying to myself, "Hmmm, somebody is going to get hurt today."

A wiser, less-stubborn person would have walked off the court then without waiting to catch a ball in one's . . . person.

I left furious. Walked out. Took my marbles and went home.

The last time someone got hurt, someone muttered half in jest, "Oh, it was my old hockey instincts." If I'd stayed for the rest of the game, likely I'd have been making excuses too, "Oh, it's my old martial-arts instincts."

Balled, battered, bullied, my first instinct is to kill. But we're educated, scholars and other sorts of bookworms; we are supposed to let shame do its work, to expect repentance, relieving us of the necessity for retaliation and endless cycles of counter-retaliation. So say the cultural historians whom I am busy reading.

The question is whether tinkering with the rules really matters. Since I haven't yet been able to answer that question, I haven't returned to the indoor soccer game. People say they like the indoor version better than the outdoor one: It's faster, harder, more driving.

For sure, and it's almost made us into an exclusive, young boys club. "Testosterone," said someone that day when I was still swearing and ranting.

If the desire to kill the ball and whatever stands between it and the net is deep—as deep as manhood, testosterone, cultural conditioning or whatever Adam is supposed to stand for—isn't it just pushing the river to think a mere rule can suppress manly, ball-pounding desire? Won't the kill-the-ball instinct be forever resurfacing?

Not immediately, mind you. For the next game or two, it would be kicks delivered at 50 per cent of full force. Then for the next couple of games, somewhere between 50 and

60 per cent. A week after that, 75 per cent, edging toward 82.3 per cent. Right? The problem is not with the rules but the ethos, the sensibility, the atmosphere, the attitude.

The other day, I heard my 10-year-old son and 12-year-old daughter wrangling.

"The boys are ball hogs," she complained after a volleyball game. "They always want the girls to get out of the way or to set them up so they can spike."

"Well, why not, boys are better players," objected my son.

"No, they're not," countered my daughter, "and even if they are, how will girls ever get better if boys don't pass the ball to them?"

At the beginning of prof ball, there were several women. Count them now.

At the beginning of the season, warm-ups took the form of a big circle, everyone passing to everyone else. The implicit aim seemed to be that of keeping the ball moving. We still see remnants of that earlier model, but a new one is displacing it: slam the ball into the wall, punch a hole in the back of the net.

What I liked about the original premise was that it was essentially co-operative, only secondarily competitive. It recognized that there we were attempting to play in a way that respected differing abilities, ages, motivations and genders. And it was play. But soon it was becoming work, serious sacrificial work.

I am told—and in good sabbatical-scholar fashion am trying to verify—that in ancient Aztec ball games, the winners earned the right to be sacrificed. As I understand it, they were allowed to have their living hearts offered to the gods. Eternal beings require strong meat. Now that's my idea of good, clean guy fun.

So I propose a new rule, much more interesting than Will's. Full repentance is a cheap shot, a quasi-Christian derivative. So instead of hooting "Shame" and extracting repentance, let us honour our deceased but more spirited neighbours to the far south and require a bodily offering of the winners, those who most successfully and flamboyantly pound balls.

But let us not be rigid or dogmatic. Let us offer the winner a choice.

There is no reason to insist that the heart is the most sacred part of the anatomy.

*Ronald L. Grimes*
Waterloo, Ont.

# A DIFFERENT KIND
# OF THOUGHT FOR FOOD

It was 8 o'clock on a Saturday morning when I put the chips-and-dip down and decided to go on a 24-hour fast. Having just finished a book on meditation, I was feeling spiritually enlightened; now that my soul was cleansed, it was time to cleanse my body.

The first few hours were relatively easy. I managed to silence the occasional perplexed grumble from my stomach with affirmations of inner strength and superiority over the non-fasting masses. But hunger, or at least the desire to eat, grew rapidly, and at hour six my stomach emitted a thunderous roar of indignation. Had I ever deprived myself of food for so long? Certainly, but only while asleep and never with the prospect of eating so distant.

By hour eight, all thoughts led to food and all trips led to the kitchen. I was listless, crabby, unabashedly famished. Fears of heart failure and malnutrition set in. I felt a migraine coming on; hallucinations were imminent. I devoured two aspirin, a multivitamin and two chewable vitamin C tablets—an exquisite but altogether inadequate meal. At 4 p.m., I went back to bed.

An hour later I mustered the strength to crawl out of bed and go to the hospital. Not to check myself in, although it did cross my mind, but to visit an old friend. Recently, Mrs. Fraser had suffered a severe heart attack and stroke, rendering her virtually unable to speak or move.

When I walked into the hospital room and saw her, all thoughts of food vanished. Emaciated and frail, her head thrown back over the pillow, face drawn, mouth open, tiny chest heaving, she looked like a baby bird fallen from her nest and slowly starving to death. This was not the spry old woman I remembered.

I was four years old when Mr. and Mrs. Fraser moved into our neighbourhood. They were the friendliest, most good-natured couple I would ever meet. I visited them regularly, sometimes with my mother or siblings, occasionally with neighbourhood kids, often alone. Mrs. Fraser loved company. She would prop me up at her kitchen table by the window, where the yellow curtains gave the illusion of perpetual sunshine and out would come heaps of food: little sandwiches, cheese, olives, pickles, tea and her delicious homemade cookies. The two of us would nibble and chatter for hours.

Over the years, an unusual, special friendship evolved. She was old enough to be my grandmother, yet she never treated me like a little boy and I never treated her like an old lady. When I turned 19, I moved to the city, but I still dropped by for visits when I could. Every Valentine's Day she sent a card to my office, signing it "from your secret admirer," gleefully aware of the gossip it incited among my colleagues.

Later in life Mrs. Fraser encountered health problems, family tragedies and, when Mr. Fraser was admitted to a seniors' home, loneliness. But she never complained. She was more concerned about the welfare of others. Generous and fiercely independent, she supported a cornucopia of charities, drove herself to church every Sunday and contin-ued to open her home to friends, neighbours, those in need. During my visits her hardships were apparent not in her attitude, which was always stubbornly optimistic, but in the snacks she served: The cookies were no longer homemade but store-bought, I started making the tea, sometimes there were no snacks at all.

Now, as I approached this formidable old woman in her hospital bed, I could see little evidence of that indomitable spirit. She looked defeated. I sat down next to her and took her hand. Her eyes, fierce and panic-stricken, darted around the room before resting on me. Then they lit up, and I recognized the old friend I'd known and loved for 30 years.

An orderly dropped off a dinner tray: grey, minced turkey, mushy vegetables, dry rice. To me, now 10 hours into my fast, it looked delicious. But my days of being fed by Mrs. Fraser were over: It was time for me to feed her.

She opened her mouth as I held each forkful out, closing her eyes as she swallowed, wincing, sometimes dribbling, sometimes breaking into a fit of coughing. After a few forkfuls she clamped her mouth shut. All the joy in eating was gone; it was just too much effort. The strawberry ice cream was better received and although the tea was lukewarm and weak, she drank it spoonful by spoonful until it was gone.

I asked her if she enjoyed the meal. She opened her mouth, struggling to speak, and out came two raspy words that I had heard her say often, words that epitomized her spirit: "You bet." I smiled and took her hand, and sat with her until her eyelids grew heavy with sleep and her grip fell away.

On the way home my appetite returned, but not in its former voracious, take-a-bite-out-of-the-dashboard state.

Sadness for my friend had tamed it; my hunger felt peaceful, appropriate.

The next morning, as I ended my fast by feasting on everything I could get my hands on, I tried to think of the starving people in the world, people who would likely be appalled by this dramatization of a mere 24-hour fast. But I could only think of Mrs. Fraser: someone who, like me, had probably never gone hungry a day in her life.

Two weeks later she stopped eating. The hospital staff didn't put her on IV; there was no point. Still, she held on for almost a week.

On April 27, after a lifetime of feeding others, of nourishing us with tea and cookies, conversation and inspiration, Mrs. Fraser died. Not of starvation, although it probably did speed up the process, but of old age.

How lucky for me that I will probably meet the same fate.

*Daniel E. Craig*
Vancouver, B.C.

## CELEBRATING MY THIRD RE-BIRTH DAY

"Where did you get your medical training?" I asked the anesthetist.

"At the University of Edinburgh," she replied.

Those were the last words I heard as I slipped into unconsciousness. I came to about 20 hours later. I couldn't move, and could barely breathe. My arms were pinned to the hospital sheets. I had a tube up my nose, another in my neck, a third in my arm and yet another in my mouth. My head was immobilized.

I'd never been happier in my life. I was awake, Ergo, I was alive.

When I awoke, I had a dull, numb pain in my abdomen, a discomfort that I've come to live with (and to treasure) since that day: May 1, 1998. I was another successful statistic—one of about 50 people to have received a liver transplant at the Toronto General Hospital that year. In an unusually busy week, I was one of three liver transplantees.

In the transplant recovery ward, there were about another dozen people who had received other organs—kidneys, hearts, lungs, pancreases—in the preceding week, plus another 20 or so either in long-term recovery, awaiting a transplant or returning following complications arising from their operations.

I remained in intensive care for about a day, and was then moved to what's called a step-down unit. That period is foggy in my memory, as I was under heavy medication and would slip in and out of hallucinatory sleep.

What I do recall with total clarity was breaking down every time visitors appeared because I was so happy to see them. In time, I was moved into a regular room in the ward, where I remained for three weeks dealing with a string of minor complications. I had a never-ending parade of doctors, residents, nurses, food servers, physiotherapists, pharmacists, orderlies and cleaning staff coming to my room. I rarely slept because of the bi-hourly drug regimen, the pain of bedsores and the sheer exhilaration of being alive. As I regained my strength, I roamed the transplant recovery unit through the night, pushing my intravenous machine, and pausing at the nurses' station to chat. During the day, there was a constant stream of visitors. On May 15 of that year, my wife and I celebrated our 27th anniversary by ordering in Chinese food from the same restaurant that we had ordered from the night after we were married. I was released a week later, and convalesced at home.

I have Hepatitis C. I contracted it when I was five weeks old, when inoculated against smallpox in unsanitary conditions in Poland immediately after the Second World War. The virus remained somewhat dormant until I was 40, and I didn't know that I had been living with it until it was discovered during a routine physical examination. Soon the virus progressed and I contracted cirrhosis. I was told by my hepatologist (liver specialist) that there was no antidote, that I would have about five years to live and that my only chance of survival was a liver transplant.

As my condition deteriorated, I entered the transplant clinic at the Toronto Hospital. I learned that I was a good candidate for a transplant because my blood type,

AB-positive, made me a universal recipient. I was placed on the transplant list and given a beeper, in case I could not be reached by telephone. The wait began.

Just before midnight on April 30, 1998, I was watching an NBA playoff game and eating pineapple. I was always eating in those days, even though I was on an extremely restricted diet, because my failing organs ignored or rejected the food I kept offering my struggling body. The phone rang. Told to report to emergency in two hours, I was there in 30 minutes. Through the early hours of the morning, I was given a battery of tests while the staff waited for the new liver to arrive. Actually, the liver I received was used, but I was assured that it was in mint condition. Securing the liver was no simple matter. The transplant clinic had received a call that an AB-positive liver was available in another Canadian city. A surgeon and a resident fellow flew there, harvested the liver and brought it back to Toronto in a matter of hours. By noon, I was speaking to the anesthetist.

In the year 2000, 712 organ transplants from 351 donors were performed in Ontario. Approximately half the donors are living. But, currently, there are about 1,600 persons on the waiting list in Ontario, and many of them will not be as fortunate as I have been. The need for organs is growing, but the supply is diminishing.

People are dying because the public is poorly informed. Transplantation myths abound. These include the mistaken views that there are widespread religious prohibitions, that organs are donated to those with wealth and influence, and that there is a ready supply. In fact, transplantation is encouraged by major religions. Selections are based on need and compatibility of blood and/or tissue type and less than 2 per cent of deaths occur in such a way as to make organ donation a possibility. Organ donation is confidential and does not limit funeral options, and organ retrieval is carried out with respect and dignity to the donor.

I will soon celebrate my third re-birthday. This date has become far more significant for me and my family than my original birthday: without being given a second chance, there would be no birthday of any kind to celebrate. I am eternally grateful to thousands of people, most of whose names I do not know. They include doctors, scientists and healthcare workers.

Most of all, I am indebted to donor X, who chose to sign a donation card, or to his or her family, who made a difficult decision during a terrible moment.

Otherwise, I would not be writing these words.

*Frank Bialystok*
Toronto, Ont.

# THE JOYS AND SORROWS
# OF OWNING A BIG RIG

We were saddened when our 1992 Kenworth truck was sold to the local wrecker.

We patted it goodbye, but my husband, Bob, scanned the wrecking yard every time we drove past for a look at his truck. Our future in trucking had gone up in a puff of black engine smoke and only $12,000 to $18,000 would fix it. Impossible. We were still paying on previous repairs.

We missed the truck. No matter if the hood was up and broken parts were being replaced, or flat tires were being fixed by the repair guy, it still sat proudly in the driveway. It was a big white beacon calling its driver to roll on down the highway. Its very presence said, "Load up, we've got places to go!" And go we did.

Despite the troubles, we had many good times in the truck. Most of Bob's runs were border crossings on the eastern seaboard, hauling, among other things, paper and nylon fibres to Georgia and South Carolina. Back hauls could be anything from pickles to fabric. When he signed on with a deck company, he went westward to Winnipeg and Edmonton. He even made the stretch in mid-winter to Snow Lake in northern Manitoba.

The Kenworth had two air-ride seats that really bounced back and forth going over the mountains in Pennsylvania. It felt like riding a horse—maybe I should have been yelling "Yahoo!" out the window. It had enough engine power to keep hauling heavy loads of snowmobiles or water pipes up long, steady slopes. And enough braking power to stop us from slamming into whatever building was sitting right at those curves at the bottom of two-mile hills. Why on earth do they build things there?. Don't they feel the slightest bit nervous as those headlights come racing toward the front window?

Many truckers like to have company on their runs. Bob would be away for a few days or up to a couple of months. The truck became his home away from home. Whenever possible, one or the other of our two sons or I travelled for a week or two at a time with him. Those trips were working vacations that let us see just how lucky we are in eastern Ontario. Our sons were allowed time from school for their trips because there was so much to learn.

Several American printing plants permit drivers to see how things work. They would talk about how they produce many magazines at one place, and how newspapers fly through the printing presses. One son came home with a bundle of National Geographic magazines, nature books and a couple of colouring books. Other factories, for safety reasons mostly, will not let anyone in—not even to use a bathroom when there isn't another loo around for miles.

Truck travel is not what one would call, um . . . luxurious. We didn't see the touristy stuff. Most of our trip nights were spent parked at truck stops, sleeping in the "cosy" single-sized truck bunk. The big plazas welcome weary truckers with showers and fresh towels (free with fuel purchase of 250 litres at many spots) and all-night restaurants with bountiful food.

Since I was not a regular passenger, the sound of trucks coming and going so near to us in the parking lot made me think we were about to be slammed into. Thank heavens that never happened. I gradually learned to sleep through the chugging of engines and the whirring of air conditioners.

Security officers patrolled the bigger parking areas. Truckers are targets for thieves, and security allows them to relax for a while. In any season, millions of dollars' worth of shining, beautiful trucks and their loads would sit there each night. I had to stick close to my hubby or I would never find our truck in row-upon-row of trucks and trailers headed for destinations across the continent.

The world away from home was fascinating. Our sons saw highway construction that used the latest and biggest in equipment. "Big Bertha" is the name of one huge excavator that could just about scoop up the whole truck into its bucket. Both sons saw the seamier sides of New York; only one saw the rough and dangerous dockyards. The youngest saw our own East Coast and the Atlantic Ocean. The older son viewed the Arizona desert and cacti just a few weeks later.

I was surprised at the diversity of the southern states, particularly South Carolina. The summer shoreline was green and leafy and the interior, only a few miles away, was sweltering, arid and brown. An upscale brick mansion may be surrounded by unpainted clapboard shacks whose yards are filled with children and dogs. Churches cropped up everywhere.

On one trip to North Carolina we found time to stop at a motel for the night. We found one that looked decent, with a pool, and had room to park the truck. We thought it would be great to have a dip after roasting all day. No such luck. That pool, and every one on the strip, had algae blooms due to unseasonably hot weather. Sigh. It was good to stretch out on a proper bed, anyway.

Travelling by truck enabled us to see cities and areas we would otherwise never have visited. It also meant that there were breakdowns almost every month. Tires blew, water pumps went (three of them) and transmissions mashed gears. All time-consuming, all expensive.

It is difficult to find carriers that are able to keep their owner/operators moving steadily. Skyrocketing fuel prices, large repair bills, truck payments and other overhead costs make trucking a hard way to earn a living. From our unhappy business experience, we don't recommend buying a big rig. Find a good employer that allows riders. Take your family and friends.

Enjoy the ride.

*Susanna McLeod*
Kingston, Ont.

## CONVERSATIONS WITH MY CAR

I don't know why I feel compelled to talk to my car.

Clearly, the car has no intention of talking back. Furthermore, even if my car does have a personality (which of course it doesn't) then I'm quite certain that we wouldn't have much in common.

The car is a white-on-rust '88 Buick Regal (LTD). It has a fuzzy blue interior, a digital speedometer that converts to mph from km/h with the click of a button (there are many buttons, but this one is bigger than most) and nowhere to put your coffee. It was a true Bubby-mobile, being my friend's grandmother's car until she was unable to drive it anymore or something. I don't really know how the family received it, but they were glad to sell. It is not an attractive machine. However, I am becoming increasingly fond of it and tell it as much if ever we're alone.

There are at least two ways I might talk to my car. The first doesn't really count, an epithet-loaded stress-relieving diatribe delivered on cold mornings when the door-lock won't even open. Kind of like a pedestrian getting mad at slush, it assumes nothing of the listener's ability to comprehend.

The other conversations, though, are a little bit more private. I talk to my car as though it's a person with feelings. Not someone I'm super-close to (I don't know if the car is a boy or a girl, for example) but someone with more personality than sheet metal should allow.

For example, I thank the car at the end of a particularly gruelling drive for doing such a good job, and might apologize for driving around with the handbrake on or some similarly unnecessary torture.

I have done this all my life. As a kid, I always loved my bicycle, and talked to it often. Back then, I knew it was a silly habit that I ought to grow out of, although I never did and I still talk to my bike today. I love my bike.

And it's not just vehicles of transportation with whom I'll hold court. I talk to lots of things, come to think of it. And I'm quite sure it's not cool to do so. We live in a loft on Queen Street, the epicentre of cool in Toronto, and other tenants in our building don't appear to wonder aloud if their apartment missed them when they were gone for the holidays.

How simplistic is my psyche? Sheesh. Or better yet, how simplistic is yours?

I'm not going to go out on a limb all by myself here; I'm bringing you with me. Everyone has similar relationships to objects in their lives, and it is patently ridiculous.

I mean it.

Perhaps you can justify ascribing a personality to small beings with dubious emotional capacity (pet fish for example, or the houseplants) but it's tricky to allow the same leniency in talking to your favourite golf club every time you see him.

Perhaps it's considered okay to talk to various manmade objects under certain circumstances. Perhaps a spirit-force of some kind occupies the souls of all inanimate beings, and is pleased that I talk to hotdogs and believe I can make them happier by eating them. But I don't think so.

The metaphysical implications of all those hotdogs sitting in stores waiting patiently for me to arrive is so ridiculous that a far more likely conclusion must be realized: I am playing the fool for all this empty chatter.

It may be understandable behaviour on a desert island, but it is not rational.

I don't think it's all harmless, either. How much stuff are we all holding onto because we don't want to hurt any feelings? Do you really think your stuffed bear has feelings? I know someone whose home is bursting at the seams with all the items she's holding onto.

Is that person you?

Well. Through years of diligence, I've restricted the bulk of the talking to within my own head (although I admit it's not as satisfying as saying the words out loud).

I will continue to talk to my car, and I'm sure that you will continue to talk to the things in your life as well.

It's probably normal human behaviour, after all.

Too bad it isn't cool.

*Tom Hannam*
Toronto, Ont.

# FOES AND FEARS

## CLOSE CALLS, DOGS AND HORSESHOES

The temperature was near freezing (or melting, depending on your perspective) and the sidewalk snowplow had spent the afternoon in my neighbourhood clearing walkways that homeowners had neglected to shovel.

The city had been covered in a thick blanket of snow that had arrived steadily over several days. City staff were working hard to get caught up with removal duties but sidewalks were a lower priority than streets. Up to this point, walking had been challenging and downright dangerous in places, so my foot-travel had been restricted to required trips rather than pleasure jaunts.

My dog, Stew, had found this difficult to swallow. Daily walks were an integral part of Stew's balanced life prescription.

With nothing pressing to accomplish and freshly cleared sidewalks, I leashed Stew, and we headed out the front door. The air was fresh and clear, and everything looked beautiful thanks to the glimmering white camouflage and stunning blue sky. I could feel a gentle warmth on my face from the sun. This was a winter day that was hard to resist.

We walked and walked and walked. Stew sniffed every post, shrub, tire and tree while marking our trail with her bright yellow signature. Gleefully, she buried her face in the fluffy white snow. The part-husky of her loved winter and, today, she was in her glory. I found her enthusiasm contagious, so extended our walk down less familiar streets, enjoying the new turf and having a wonderful afternoon with my canine friend.

When the winter sun began losing its heat, I started to weave us back home. My route brought us to a busy artery street at the end of my block, midway between traffic lights. Rush hour was just cranking up. The stream of cars plus the fading sun was all it took to replace my afternoon calm with a sense of urgency. My thoughts skipped ahead with questions. What would we have for dinner? Would the kids be home from school yet? Was Ian getting the car emissions test today? Suddenly, I had things to do, people to see and time was ticking. I decided that rather than walk the two blocks in either direction for a controlled intersection, I would save time by crossing right where I was.

I have read statistics that claim most traffic accidents happen within one kilometre of a person's home. Familiar territory has a tendency to lull one into a false sense of security and people forget the importance of what they are doing and start planning ahead. It would seem that I had fallen into that category.

The heavy, end-of-day traffic slowed and eventually stopped for the red light farther down the street. Before stepping off the sidewalk, I spotted the car I wanted to cross in front of and made direct eye contact with the driver of that car. I cinched Stew closer to my right side and started moving so that I could get a clear view of oncoming traffic. The next several seconds are permanently etched in my mind.

I had forgotten about the second lane of traffic. As I looked right, another car came zooming toward the intersection from my left. Someone honked their horn in warning and I instinctually leaned back just in time for the car to brush my coat and narrowly miss my feet. Stew was not so lucky. Her head was sticking out past my legs and with a whack that sounded like a baseball being struck, her nose met the bumper of the car.

My horrified reaction was instant. I pulled her to the sidewalk and dropped to my knees. Blood was dripping from her nostrils and a large bump was forming on the left side of her nose. She was licking furiously, shaking all over, her eyes wild with fear. I checked her mouth and teeth; then I gathered some snow and laid it on her face. She leaned against me and I held her close.

The Whack! sound of bumper meeting dog nose rang in my ears. I shuddered to think . . . A single second and a couple of centimetres seemed the only separation between what happened and what might have happened.

After my heart rate lowered, with extreme caution we continued down our street, stopping every few metres to rest. I examined Stew further and found no additional injury. The serene beauty I had basked in earlier that afternoon had vanished and Stew's joyousness had ceased. My mind was blank except for the single thought of getting us home.

To my knowledge, I have never come that close to the edge of life. I was not on a life-threatening quest that afternoon. No skydiving for this girl. My near-life-ending act was one that I had successfully performed hundreds of times in the past. I guess I was successful on this occasion, too, but only just.

When I got home, Ian asked me never to leave the house again. This was a funny idea and one that felt perfectly reasonable for the time being. I wanted to wrap myself in a blanket and crawl up on his lap. I had the urge to cry but I never found any tears.

The following morning, Stew's nose was cold and wet as she sat happily on her porch chair, surveying the streetscape and snoozing the morning away. With the exception of the bump, she seemed unscathed.

For me, something had shifted. I felt a pulsing heat in my body core that was quite unlike my typical winter state. I was alert to the point of bursting with excitement, energy and a desire to do something marvellous, something that I've been putting off, something new and meaningful.

They say that close only counts in horseshoes and hand grenades but perhaps close counts in brushes with death, too.

Sue *Richards*
Guelph, Ont.

# THE TYRANNY OF WELLNESS AS METAPHOR

In January of the new millennium, I was diagnosed with cancer. Okay, so it was only thyroid cancer, which Jay Teitel of *Toronto Life* has so aptly nicknamed "stupid" cancer because it spreads so slowly. It is also the easiest cancer to treat, with only a minor chance of recurring. The irony is that although it was comforting to know that my prognosis was excellent, I still found myself stumbling down the thorny psychological paths frequented by those struck with more serious forms of cancer.

Like an expectant mother who begins to tune into the maternal world that was once overlooked, all of a sudden I felt surrounded by this dreaded disease. First, there was the tragic passing of Sandra Schmirler, who just happened to be the same age as me, followed by CBC Magazine's documentary series on the ongoing search for the cure. And every magazine I picked up featured an article on a heroic cancer patient.

Perhaps it was a knee-jerk reaction on my part, but I found these portraits in courage off-putting. I questioned the value of these deliberate attempts to tug at our collective heart strings, like all those Hollywood movies in which cancer is the co-star.

After discovering that Susan Sontag was battling cancer for the second time, I decided to reread *Illness as Metaphor*, which Sontag wrote in 1978 after her first battle with cancer. This time it was like a balm, an antidote to the sentimentality, mixed messages and inner turmoil I was experiencing.

In *Illness as Metaphor*, Sontag strives to free us from the punitive or sentimental fantasies about mysterious illnesses such as tuberculosis, cancer and mental illness. In her essay, she demonstrates that throughout history—in medical practice, literature and folk wisdom—serious disease and sickness have been assigned all kinds of meaning that in actual fact have nothing to do with the disease. More recently, thanks to the legacy of Freud, cancer victims were believed to be suffering from the results of repression. In other words, like the title of one of her other famous works, Sontag makes a strong case "against interpretation."

I, too, have hit upon an idea. This idea springs from a combination of my personal encounter with cancer and my reflections on *Illness as Metaphor*. It is my firm conviction that wellness as metaphor is just as prevalent as its flipside.

Like illness, wellness is charged with meaning, especially in today's health-conscious society. We don't just want good health but perfect health. This is indicative of our excessive drive for perfection. It is also part of the conspicuous consumption that surrounds us. Our obsession with both physical and psychological health is part of our craving for control, an offshoot of an affluent society's lack of perspective about serious problems. We have forgotten that the human organism doesn't have to be perfect to be deemed healthy. Good health includes all sorts of malfunctions, abnormalities and even some forms of sickness.

Until my encounter with cancer, I tended to take my wellness for granted. I have never abused my body in any way, but I have not taken much of a proactive approach, either. When I was first diagnosed with cancer, however, I suddenly felt guilty about my lifestyle, wondering what I had done to set it off. I attribute my guilt trip to recent trends that accentuate a patient's role both in causing and curing his or her own disease. We are instructed to monitor our diets and to adopt a positive frame of mind, as though the disease can be conquered by sheer force of will. The message is clear: failure to comply will result in a relapse and then it will be your own fault.

Upon reflection, I realized that my guilt trip was unwarranted: it wasn't my fault that I had cancer. Getting cancer is like winning, or rather losing, the lottery. You don't even have to enter to win, your number just comes up. This idea is not as flippant and simplistic as it seems. By adopting this attitude, I am not denying the proven links between a healthy lifestyle and prolonged good health. On the other hand, cancer is a supremely complicated disease that should not be reduced to whether or not you ate enough broccoli. But that is precisely how some of the cancer-related literature makes it sound.

Cancer can be caused by any number of factors: environmental, genetic, social and dietary. My lottery image is not a dismissal of these serious issues. Rather, cancer remains a mystery: it is unpredictable and beyond our control.

In *Illness as Metaphor*, Sontag boldly declares illness is not a metaphor. I would like to add to that: neither is wellness. And yet, as in less-enlightened times, there is a trend to regard good health as a reflection of the individual. The old puritan adage, "cleanliness is next to godliness," has been replaced with "fitness is next to godliness."

Poor health is not a punishment for bad behaviour or poor character. Contrary to current thinking, the pursuit of good health is not a virtue. In some ways, the pursuit of perfect health can be read as an indicator of inner moral decay: It demonstrates self-absorption and vanity more than moral righteousness.

Good health is not a birthright, it is a bonus. Perfect health is not an end in itself; it is not a lifetime achievement. "She kept herself in good shape" and "He led a healthy lifestyle" are not fitting epitaphs. Sontag's now-famous introduction claims, "Everyone who is born holds dual citizenship in the kingdom of the well and in the kingdom of the sick. Although we prefer to use only the good passport, sooner or later each of us is obliged, at least for a spell, to identify ourselves as citizens of that other place."

The key words in Sontag's introduction are "sooner or later." Could it be that contemporary culture's obsession with perfect health is a manifestation of a collective denial of the inevitability of illness and another timeless aspect of the human condition—the fear of our mortality? If so, how ironic that so much living is being wasted staving off death.

*Christine Arthurs*
Toronto, Ont.

## KNOWING AND NEEDING THE ENEMY

I have seen the life-prolonging effects of ill will.

Years ago, growing up in a small, northern New York hamlet, I watched as two old friends had a huge falling-out from a bet on the outcome of the 1960 U.S. Presidential election.

The two elderly gentlemen stopped speaking to one another. In effect, they became enemies. But this seemingly sad parting of the ways actually provided them with the motivation to live well into their 80s.

Both men had vegetable gardens and both men plied my mother with produce in a fierce competition. This war of the gardens and other silent battles gave both men a reason to persevere and to outlast their foe.

In short, having an enemy likely prolonged their lives.

One needs enemies. It seems counterintuitive, but it's true. For all the nasty prose that's been written about these hateful foes, they serve a most useful purpose.

When we were young, we were taught the golden rule: Do unto others as you would have them do unto you. We were urged to be nice to everyone and to avoid creating adversaries.

It's a common theme in the major religions of the world: Love your fellow beings even if they harm you. Turn the other cheek. Fight hatred with love and forgiveness.

But is this natural or even desirable? How much easier to give in to one's instinctive desires and work up a good hate for your adversary.

Over time, experience teaches us that the golden rule has a corollary: Do unto others before they do unto you. In other words, you need enemies.

As we get older, we need motivators to help us carry on. When your joints ache, your skin sags and your head hurts, you need a reason to live.

Perhaps the best and most powerful of these motivators is your enemy. What better reason to get out of bed in the morning? Nothing gets you up and moving like the possibility of revenge. Think about it: You haven't lived if you don't have at least one or two enemies. To have none is to deny the vitality of human life. To push the boundaries, test the limits and challenge social norms is to inevitably cross paths with someone on a contrary journey. A purpose in life necessarily means creating an enemy.

Oftentimes, you are known by your enemies. Having them can even impart a measure of status. Think of the famous enemies list kept by Richard Nixon during his dark days in The White House. Among the liberal establishment, being on that list was a badge of honour.

What about those in pursuit of noble goals, you say? Surely they have no enemies? But of course they do. To be truly dedicated to grand purposes means being an agent for change. And being an agent for change means challenging the status quo. And challenging the status quo means stepping on the toes of its guardians. *Voilà.* Instant enemies.

That's not to say that pursuing noble goals and whatever you perceive to be the greater good is pointless. Quite the contrary. It fuels the collective soul of mankind.

Just remember that the pursuit of good has a dark side, too. The thesis that one should pursue the greater good generates the antithesis that one must have enemies. To take on the powers-that-be necessarily creates foes. Luckily, in a kind of adversarial dialectic, these two propositions generate the synthesis of human progress.

To take on the abusive employer. To challenge the human rights violator. To fight for that halfway house in a residential neighbourhood. All of these actions engender resistance and hostile opponents.

You push the boundaries. The boundaries push back. And before you know it you're in a hell of a battle with someone you can't stand.

It's been said that "we can learn even from our enemies." But, in fact, we learn especially from our enemies. They provide the ethical and metaphysical mirror that shows us what we truly believe.

The real golden truism rule is not "love thine enemy." Rather, it's "know thine enemy." For if you figure out what makes your nemesis tick, you've gone a long way to knowing yourself.

So embrace your enemies. They help define who and what you are. Where would Wellington have been without his Napoleon? Or Churchill without his Hitler? Or even Superman without Lex Luthor?

Let's face it: you can't make an omelette without breaking a few eggs. And you can't get what you want without creating a few foes. So wear their existence as a badge of honour and a clear indication that you're on the right track.

If nobody hates you, you must be doing something wrong.

*David Martin*
Ottawa, Ont.

# WHEN MODESTY IS SHOCKING

For more than six months I have been living in the city of Riyadh, where, in a week, a month, probably a whole year, I will never see a woman's clothes. Instead, I see women sheathed in black *abayas*. Everywhere: on streets, in stores, riding with their husbands in fancy cars, they are covered, obliterated, "long, pyramid-like, black forms," as my 14-year-old son put it. Shadowy mysteries. And when they do not cover themselves, the religious police—for the propagation of virtue and the elimination of vice—yell at them, "Woman, cover!" and, to avoid trouble, we men quickly ask our wives and daughters to cover.

"There are people underneath those cloaks," says my boy, "real people who have lives, and they aren't allowed to express themselves." That's right, I tell him, for we are liberals. We are Canadians.

So my family was amazed to stumble into a ritzy downtown hotel in Riyadh's heart not long ago and discover a hidden world. *Abayas* were off and Western women sat lounging in clothes, laughing, chatting, in reds, greens, yellows . . . their hair exposed. It was a taste of what we enjoy in almost every other country in the world. We relaxed.

And then, an anomaly, as two Saudi "pyramids" entered the sanctuary, floated past us, sat down near us and quietly slipped their veils and *hejabs* off. From a male standpoint, it was thrilling to see. Arab women exposing the forbidden, their striking and meticulously cared-for faces. I sat transfixed like a teenager with a crush. I felt privileged and excited. It was as good as nudity. And, as a male, I rapidly understood the appeal of having women covered. I got it. Women cover here so that when they are not covered, men can get turned on.

It isn't fair to enforce women to be modest, this I know, but males do it in degrees all over the globe, in every culture, even North American. Living here, I have nostalgia for modesty now. A face can do to me now what nudity used to and I am guilty, at least at a purely sexual level, of liking this bizarre practice of cloaking women.

Males everywhere want to simultaneously see it all and cover it all—insisting on both modesty and impiety at once in their women. A 30-year revolt against these attitudes has resulted in the desexualizing of both genders in the West. In our de-ruled Western culture, norms have blurred. How does one be a man today, or a woman?

Quite often I am confused or angered by all the flesh I see in the West. I don't get sexually aroused in Western life anymore, not often, not like when I see a pair of eyes looking at me through the slit in a Saudi woman's veil. Not like I did when that woman in the hotel restaurant let me see her forehead, and five inches beyond that, her hair, framing her pretty face and her glowing skin.

Modesty made me excited. Her modesty, which she, by choice, had violated in public. Yet in Canada, where modesty is merely a quaint, retro joke, is it possible to be immodest anymore without being naked? Sure, Canadian men and women enjoy political freedoms far more important and significant than here. Women cannot even drive cars in Saudi Arabia. And I know that Gwen Jacobs did a good thing to help make us equal when she went to court for the right to go topless in public—and won. But we haven't learned in the West that gender is larger than anatomy and that sexual attraction and desirability are mysteries diminished by so much skin. If we could learn it, would we be less free?

Admittedly I am guilty of romanticizing the Saudi form of forced modesty. Forced on women here by a complicated blend of male sexual control, religion, history and culture, a mix that will likely keep Saudi women locked for decades in what I see as a strange, non-Western, quasi-freedom. I don't see things changing here, but I wouldn't presume to claim that they should.

Soon enough I will return to Canada and walk the streets. It may, for a while, be an eye-popping thrill, but I will always know that over here, women, under male control, have the potential to excite me just as much by revealing only their eyes or face, only the front of their dress, as their *abaya* splits apart on a too-fast corner or from a sudden gust of wind, and I see the forbidden flash of an ankle. The Saudi's extraordinary brand of forced modesty is a potent sexual pleasure. My little secret as I walk down the street. An appreciation I've acquired living here.

I cannot justify this male oppression, but I will admit that, for now, my maleness is pleased to see *less* of a woman. And I know that many of the world's Muslim women prefer the freedom and anonymity of being covered. Certainly my adolescent daughter has enjoyed it. In some strange way, in Saudi, the allure and mystery of covering has become intermingled with a kind of female power common to an earlier, younger West that I now only remember. Sadly, the freedom Canadian women, and men, have fought to achieve—the freedom to bare all—leaves us somehow diminished.

*Dave Clark*
Cobourg, Ont.

## TODAY, IT'S THE MEMORY OF KEYS

Yesterday it was my wallet. On any given day it could be the cell phone, a treasured fountain pen or my sunglasses. Visa bills on weekdays. Household tools needed for a crucial repair on weekends.

Today, it's the keys. They're gone.

At different times, I have blamed the nanny for moving them, the kids for playing with them, the neighbours for borrowing them and my wife for actually putting them where they're supposed to be. I have cursed the mythical key gnomes for hiding them, and would have screamed at the dog for burying them, if we had one.

But it's usually me who's to blame. And only me.

I have put something down and it has vanished into thin air. Or much worse, I have put it in a "safe place" so I won't lose it, but can't exactly remember where that place is.

"Where are the keys, dear?" politely asks my wife.

"Ahhhh. . ." I mumble with an air of desperation. "They're in a safe place," I say, implicitly acknowledging that the battle of the sexes has been resoundingly lost, along with the keys.

"A safe place" in my house is a dreaded oxymoron. It is neither safe nor a place. Like a creature of new-age Zen physics, the safe place defies all logic and reason by existing and not existing, at the same time and in the same place. The safe place occupies space and time but at different times and in different spaces, in something analogous to a twilight zone created especially for my keys. Quantum physicists, science fiction writers and Dancing Wu Li Masters would have no trouble finding the safe place using particle accelerators, yogic flying and The Force. But I cannot. My keys are in this parallel universe of un-being.

This morning, I put the keys "here" to be safe. But like Bill Clinton on the witness stand, it all depends on what you mean by "here." When I look here, the keys are not here. And they are not there either. So I spend an inordinate amount of time looking here and there: opening drawers, closing closets, checking pockets and even checking my left hand.

Fortunately, Zen reveals all: They are here and yet not here at the same time. They exist and yet they do not exist. They are in the "safe place."

You must believe me when I tell you I have an excellent memory. I can remember the smell of an old rail car from a trip across Canada I took as a six-year-old boy; the meals eaten at restaurants I visited in Europe when I was 12; the precise layout of the house I grew up in; the names of school friends I haven't seen in 35 years; places I have visited; times I have had; words spoken and heard in anger and joy.

But I suppose, like Proust, I have remembered far too much of this sort of thing.

There's a lot of trivial information I have remembered that has no apparent purpose at all. For example, a fellow soccer Dad is regularly impressed that I can recite the Architect's Skit from *Monty Python* for a full minute during off-field socializing. A lawyer friend in Toronto, who's active in the Greek community, is astonished that I could remember that the fall of Constantinople happened May 29, 1453 (a Tuesday, by the way), signalling the end of the Eastern Roman Empire. And a woman I knew a lifetime ago is absolutely thrilled that I would remember her 40th birthday and send a card.

But I cannot remember where I put my keys.

My doctor has told me not to worry. I'm in middle age now, and in middle age, you've got to expect that your memory, your colon and your libido don't function nearly as well as they did when you were 25. He tells me I am forced to remember far too much in my professional life for my own good and little things like the keys just get crowded out. On his suggestion, I started taking ginkgo biloba only to find that it, like middle age, also effects the colon. Then I put the bottle in the safe place, and haven't seen it in weeks. Life's just not fair.

So I've started to imagine my failing memory as a hard drive in need of de-fragmentation. I suppose I should be deleting from my memory all that useless personal information to make room for the co-ordinates of my Visa bills, my wallet and my keys. I should purge from the corners of my mind all those old Python skits, know-it-all events from Roman history and ancient birthdays.

The problem is, the body of useless information I've accumulated through the years has become an integral part of who I am. Deleting the trivia of my life so that there's more room to remember where the keys are makes me little more than a very reliable key hook. It does nothing for my well-deserved reputation as an entertaining soccer Dad, impressive Byzantine scholar and thoughtful old flame able to bring on a smile for the price of a stamp.

There's a scene in Stanley Kubrick's *2001: A Space Odyssey* where Dave Bowman, the surviving astronaut, must shut down Hal, the wayward computer. "My mind is going," says Hal, ". . . I can feel it," as Dave turns the special keys that empty the computer's memory bank.

Given my memory lately, I've been identifying more with Hal. You see, Dave had his keys, and I still don't have mine.

But I think they're in a safe place.

Tony Wilson
Vancouver, B.C.

## HOW DO WE STOP THE BULLYING?

"Children harassing each other is getting more extreme across the country." My morning paper reported this fact Nov. 27, 2000, and it made me stop and think: Is it?

I was a child who was harassed at school. Extremely harassed. Now I am 30, an adult. How did the experience shape who I am today? If I could go back and visit the girl I was at eight, would I give her any advice? Is present-day bullying worse? Or are we just more aware because kids employ guns and suicidal solutions?

I can remember the day I started at that new school. It was 1978, and my family had moved to an affluent Toronto neighbourhood. I was excited about all the new friends I was going to meet in Grade 2. I was a happy child with many friends from kindergarten and Grade 1. I had a close, loving relationship with my parents, who had done much to nurture a healthy sense of self-esteem in me by the tender age of eight. I was a well-adjusted kid.

It must have started when my creative-writing story was selected to be in the first position on what we called the Story Board. This rattled the previous No. 1 and waves of contempt were sent forth, which I felt immediately. Then again, it might have been sparked by my purple corduroys (not the latest Adidas-trackpant Nike-runner combination). With no older siblings, I was a bit out of the loop on the fashion spectrum. Yet all-in-all, when I look back, I think it was my quiet confidence that ultimately did me in.

I remember being shocked when it started. At eight, I hadn't been exposed to grand-scale harassment up until this point in my life. With stable, kind adults as role models and friendships with other decent children, I could not have imagined that the next three years of my life would involve such hostility from other kids and such feelings of despair on my part.

By the end of Grade 2, going to school had become a nightmare of unimaginable proportions. I didn't tell anyone at first. I just kept modifying my behaviour to try and avoid the sniper fire, but nothing I did ever seemed to take me out of the spotlight. I had become the target of incessant ridicule at the hands of other 8-, 9- and 10-year-olds. It went something like this:

"The Loser has buck teeth," they would scream when I smiled. And I did. Years later, braces would correct the imperfect grin.

"The Loser has asthma and can't run in the PlayDay races," they would taunt as I sat out from sprinting. And I did. Years later, I would become an avid swimmer, jogger, skier, tennis player and general sports enthusiast.

"The Loser doesn't even have a cottage in Muskoka!" they would sneer on Friday night. And we did not. Years later, after travelling much of the world, I still do not feel the slightest urge to purchase property in Ontario cottage country.

These comments were targeted at every aspect of my person. Nothing went unnoticed. My shoes, my pencil case, my family members, the way I walked, ran, climbed the stairs . . . even the contents of my sandwich might be the subject of ridicule that could bring the house down. And always, the remarks were accompanied by mass jeering and laughter.

The girls, who were clearly the cruellest, would devise the catch phrase of the week and sing it out with gleeful jubilation when I was near. The boys, who knew me only as Loser, would implement this message with a push in the mud or a jolt on the arm, a worm in my raincoat on a rainy day, or by sending my new five-speed bike over the fence and into the ravine—never to be recovered. Yet, more painful than any of this were the rare instances when a new friend ventured into my life, only to be quickly pulled aside and given the option—Her or Us . . . with Us being the only logical choice for any child.

Did I ask my teachers for help? Maybe at first. Yet I soon realized they did not want to intervene. They encouraged me to "be tougher" and to give "tongue-lashings" of my own. That wasn't me. Even the teachers who did care (thank you, Mr. Hook) could not protect me travelling to and from school, where the kids were most aggressive. I can remember planning exit and entry strategies, designating hiding spots for recess and lunch, and even boarding school buses first so I could sit near the driver for protection.

My mother can still recount my anguish getting dressed in the mornings, asking, "What can I wear so the kids won't make fun of me today?" I pleaded with her not to call anyone's parents, knowing this would worsen my stakes considerably. I pleaded with her not to call my teachers. I now know she contacted both, only to be told that "children must learn to fend for themselves."

And so finally, after three spirit-crushing years, my parents moved me to a new school, and my life returned to normal. By Grade 7, I was class president. I never heard from any of the bullies again. I am sure I am only one of many faint memories for them.

Today, I run my own successful business and I am extremely social. I feel good about the relationships in my life, the work I do, the way I look. The impact of the bullying did not destroy my self-esteem. I was lucky. Yet, if someone is being abusive or unkind to another in my presence, they will hear about it from me in full force. I never turn a blind eye to bad treatment of myself or others. I am the first person to fight for the "loser."

However, I do tense up when I pass a grade school at recess time. The sound of children playing yard games, where they are left to govern themselves, still makes me slightly uncomfortable. It is the only time in my adult life when I feel truly uneasy. Perhaps it is in the schoolyard where adults should teach children about basic human kindness.

And if I could go back and visit that little girl who was me? I still don't know what I would tell her.

*Kirsten Will*
Toronto, Ont.

## A SUMMIT OF TWO

This began as a letter to thank Annette.

Stationed next to the Arts Centre on boulevard René-Lévesque in Quebec City on a Saturday night in April, Annette became more than a faceless member of the Sûreté du Québec. As we talked over my imminent arrest, she showed she was more than the number stencilled on her helmet. As she had always been—although it was easy to lose sight of it through all the tear gas.

This isn't to thank Annette for not arresting me. In the end that was my choice. For a while, though—standing alone at 2:30 a.m.—it seemed inevitable.

It wasn't supposed to be this way. Like the police, I hadn't even wanted to be there.

I'm not opposed to free trade. Heck, I might even support the FTAA itself, although it's too early to say. After agonizing for days I'd decided against the five-hour drive to Quebec City. Although opposed to the disdain for alternative views expressed by (some) elected officials, I thought my support for legitimate dissent might be overshadowed by other messages at the Summit.

Then I read The Globe that Saturday morning. What moved me, what brought me to tears, was the young woman staring from behind a fence. The fence. Innocent. Angry. And effectively silenced.

I knew I had no choice.

This wasn't a parade. It wasn't a party. It was dissent. Legitimate, democratic expression. It required respect. If it wasn't going to get it from politicians, it was damn well going to get it from me.

So I went to Quebec City. And the Sûreté almost arrested me.

All night, crowds had moved back and forth along boulevard René-Lévesque, with the unpredictable waves of gas spread by giant fans. A line of riot police stood, set back about 50 feet from the street, guarding approaches to the delegates beyond.

For four hours, I stood before them, feet away, along with a few other demonstrators. At times, others would pass by, thanking the police for being there. For doing their jobs.

Seriously.

Of course, violence occurred elsewhere. In addition to the gas, twice I saw the brilliant arc of Molotov cocktails.

But, near me, the protest was peaceful. Although you wouldn't know it from the gas. Every 15 minutes, clouds spread down the street, choking us. But this was a peaceful position.

By 2 o'clock, though, the Sûreté had decided to shut down the street. Most of the protesters around me had already moved—home or to more active positions.

There was no warning. The fans began. A cloud of gas drifted toward me. As it neared I pulled my bandanna over my face, bracing myself. But it was worse than I could have imagined.

Tear gas is horrific. At first, the caustic air brushes the back of your throat, burning, while your eyes start to water. A bandanna helps, but eventually the gas works its way through it into your nostrils. Into your eyes.

It burns to the point of disorientation. This time it brought me to my knees. Screaming, crying. Unable to move. An officer laughed. I thought I'd pass out.

I opened my eyes too early, once. I was deep inside a cloud. My breath came in ragged gasps through the cotton pressed against my mouth.

I had nowhere to run, even if I'd been able to stand. Police before me. Everywhere else, gas. It took an eternity. When I opened my eyes again I was alone. Except for the Sûreté.

To my right, police moved along a cross street, in lines to prevent security breaches, clearing out the remaining protesters. To my left, there was still only gas.

An officer moved forward, pointing.

"Go."

The mask filtered his voice, but the message was clear. Left or right. Always back. I had a choice.

But I'd done nothing wrong. So I stood my ground. I could hardly see.

Moments later he returned. He gestured again. Away.

Struggling with his English, he explained. If I refused to leave, the police would advance, at which point, if I didn't move, I'd be arrested and charged with obstruction of justice.

This wasn't why I was in Quebec City. But I'd done nothing wrong. So I stayed.

Blinking back tears. Waiting for the line.

Nothing happened. Not for a while.

Then Annette stepped forward. Dressed in padded green fatigues, black helmet and gas mask, she spoke flawless English. I could only see her eyes.

She asked my name and I answered. She replied in kind.

Once more she explained my options. Move or be arrested.

Again I said no.

My presence was legitimate. I posed no threat to her or to the delegates beyond.

As she returned to the line, I turned, watching two protesters behind me moving slowly, hands raised. Police with batons chased two more.

No one else moved.

Minutes later: "Chris? Have you changed your mind yet?"

It was Annette. I couldn't help but smile.

But I said no.

And so we waited.

When she returned, we talked.

I explained why I was there. That I knew she was doing her job. A legitimate job.

She understood—and respected—why I was there. She had listened. So, she said, wasn't it time to go?

As she spoke, the line to my right turned sideways and marched away, leaving just 10 officers behind. They turned to avoid walking into me—of that I have no doubt.

No one there wanted to arrest me. I'd caused them no trouble. Her words, not mine.

Yes, I understood I'd be in jail until Monday.

But I'd done nothing wrong.

In the end, pragmatism prevailed—although there's a fine line between this and cowardice, to be sure. A line I struggled with, before the weight of the police. But they had listened. And they still had a job to do.

I had one request: "Walk with me."

Annette and a colleague accompanied me. When we reached the perimeter, I turned. As the remnants of gas swirled around us, next to another line of riot police, they responded to my extended arm. But before they shook my hand, they removed their gloves.

They didn't have to do that. And that is why I'm thankful.

*Christopher K. Penny*
Wakefield, Que.

# WELCOME TO THE
# SCHOOLYARD PEACE CONFERENCE

I think that all the problems in the world could be solved if the rulers and head honchos just sat down and talked about their difficulties once they had come in from recess and finished having a snack.

A girl named Jacqueline in Grade 2 informed me of a very interesting concept called Peace Conference that she has implemented in her school in order to solve the squabbling and animosity that happens when the students venture out into the playground.

It can be a mean world for little Timmy who is constantly being picked upon by older boys. Or for Emily who is not allowed to play jump rope because she doesn't have the same hair barrette as everyone else.

When the children come in from the unforgiving pavement, grass, swings and slides, which represent their time for fun and freedom, some feel helpless and distraught because of the aggressive and commanding behaviour that some other children allow themselves to manifest.

Timmy cannot concentrate on his numbers and alphabet because he is upset about the way he was treated. Emily feels helpless and does not want to participate during class.

This causes the teacher to become frustrated because her students are unhappy and she therefore cannot teach them. It is time for a Peace Conference, and in walks Jackie: a bold seven-year-old girl with blond hair, a sympathetic grin and more wisdom for her years than you can imagine.

Jackie forfeits her snack time to go around to the classrooms to end the fighting and teasing that goes on outside. She is the leader of this conference and one of her friends is her second-in-command. (There used to be a third but he retired because he didn't like having to miss snack time.) Each class from Grade 1 to Grade 5 has a Peace Conference after recess. (Jackie is soon going to expand the conference to the portables in order to include the Grade 6's.) Peace Conference usually takes about 15 minutes and it allows students to reveal their sources of torment.

The most intriguing part about Peace Conference is that there is no name-calling or finger-pointing. For instance, Timmy is only allowed to say that he was teased during recess; he is not allowed to name the perpetrators. The people who are guilty must willingly raise their hand and admit to their wrongdoings. They will not be punished and will be praised for their voluntary confession. This concept allows the students to talk about the distress and harassment that goes on in the playground. They are able to discuss their situation openly instead of allowing it to weigh down upon them like a cumulonimbus cloud just waiting to burst.

Jackie introduced this concept to her class and then to her school; she had learned it from her Grade 1 teacher in Nova Scotia who had invented it when she realized that her students were coming in from recess upset about how they were being treated by other students. Jackie has taken this responsibility upon herself to promote a safe environment for all students and to help end the teasing, bullying and threatening that goes on.

She seems to have a solution for all scenarios. If the accused does not admit to having teased Timmy and everyone knows that he did it, even the teacher, then she will talk to witnesses and build a case in order to stop the harassment—in a dignified manner, of course. She says that once the problems have been brought out into the open, the teasing usually subsides. If her class goes a whole week without any calamities, they have a Peace Parade to celebrate the good behaviour and co-operation of the students.

Jackie also uses her negotiating skills with the children in her neighbourhood. If someone is teasing her and she has to go inside for supper, she is unable to leave the matter until another day. She can't let it go because the teasers will forget about their offensive behaviour and may even deny that they did anything at all.

Fifteen minutes is all it takes to get these problems ironed out. Some are, of course, more complex to deal with, but at least the children are able to discuss them in a compassionate environment, without allowing themselves to be drenched in self-pity with angst bubbling and boiling inside of them.

Peace Conference may seem like a way to solve only the problems of the playground, but in a sense this playground represents a miniature version of our cities, countries and our world. The children deal with similar problems, such as stealing, threatening, violence and name-calling.

On a larger scale these circumstances obviously become more severe, especially when guns replace sticks and threats are no longer threats of a punch in the face, but become threats of bombs on city buses.

It may seem impractical to assume this simple method would be able to solve the world's problems, but it couldn't hurt to try.

All we need is a seven-year-old girl named Jacqueline to tell the world leaders that they won't get punished as long as they raise their hands and admit to their wrongdoings. She will reward them with her genuine smile and the fact that they no longer have to embody the hatred and antipathy that churns inside them and, until now, could only be released by making loud noises and wreaking havoc upon the lives of innocent people.

*Angelique Myles*
Kingston, Ont.

## JUST QUIT, BABY

Quitting is good for the soul. I recommend it. And when you've mastered quitting, the next step on the road to building real character is failing—more challenging but with even greater rewards than quitting.

But quitting first: You've probably heard that "nobody likes a quitter," but just who is this "nobody" anyway and why should we care what he thinks, especially if he's "nobody"? The person to please is yourself.

I started practising quitting in high school: I quit the swim team and the orchestra because although I enjoyed swimming and music in a noncommittal kind of way, I hated both between the hours of 7 and 9 a.m. I loathed jumping into cold water before I was even awake, hated the din of stringed instruments played with no great skill or dedication before I'd even had breakfast. In fact, even history class was too early for me so I quit that, too. Instead, I spent first period at the restaurant eating bacon on a bun, drinking coffee and smoking. Now, that's the way to wake up.

However, these early forays into what was then considered pretty eccentric behaviour did not come without a price. For years afterward, I had recurring dreams about wandering the halls of my old high school looking for my locker, clutching my viola. The climax of the dream is when I remember I have to play in a concert and realize I don't know the pieces.

No doubt my highest achievement was quitting law school after earning straight A's in my first year. I quit because I don't like whatever it is that I'm doing—a job, a program of study, any kind of enterprise at all. So why did I get involved with it in the first place? Because I thought I would or might like it and I tried it out and I didn't, so I quit. Or I liked it for a while, and then I didn't, so I quit. While I've been practising the art of quitting, I've been refining my preferences, discovering my passions, developing new skills, having adventures. What if, driven by fear of quitting and failing, I had forced myself to complete law school and was now a lawyer? Sure, I'd own some nice suits (I think that was what attracted me to the profession in the first place), I'd have more job security, probably live in a bigger apartment, definitely would have more . . . yeah, but I'd also have to be at work at 7 a.m.

I know there are things you don't quit without long and hard contemplation—marriage, for example. And then there are things that you can almost never justify quitting, like being a parent. I'm not talking about quitting on people you have committed yourself to, and who rely on you. I'm talking about allowing yourself to quit the lesser commitments: jobs, careers, lovers, hobbies. Quitting has been good for me, has tested my faith in the future and my tolerance for uncertainty, and helped me develop both. While I've been quitting, I've been learning not to quit on myself.

I'd advise anybody to quit. Quit especially when you're not happy, when you find yourself complaining and are tired of your own whiny voice. Quit when people treat you badly, and quit especially when you find yourself treating other people badly. Quit for fun just to try something new. Quit to open up a space in your life—a silent, mysterious place—and wait to see what happens there.

Once you've got quitting under your belt, you're ready to graduate to failing. Now failing is strong stuff and not for everybody. Unlike quitting, which you initiate yourself and is usually cause for rejoicing, failing often comes as an unpleasant surprise. You fail despite what you think are your best efforts. You fail when someone else makes a judgment and you don't measure up. You get fired. You get dumped. A failed relationship is the most intimately painful thing there is, as anyone who has experienced it knows. And nothing beats getting fired for dismantling your self-esteem and destroying your sense of purpose and belonging.

And yet failing, too, has provided me with lessons I needed to learn which all boil down to one: I am responsible for just about everything that happens to me. When I fail, it's because I didn't want to succeed, or didn't want to enough. After all, I've succeeded at the things that were most important to me. I've paid my rent on time every single month for the past 20 years. I quit smoking. I got published in The Globe.

My failures have made me examine the source of my ambivalence and pushed me to make conscious choices. My failures have instructed me about the perils of not choosing, and spawned resolutions (whoa, I'll never do that again!) that I've kept. Through undergoing small (like the slow death of my kitchen window herb garden) and larger failures, I've been learning about what's important to me, as well as getting used to not being perfect. I've come to accept my failures as strong medicine.

Quitting and failing have made me land on my feet so many times, I am developing calluses that soon will allow me to walk over hot coals. That is the kind of preparation you need for life. You need to be ready for hot coals and loneliness and other dark nights of the soul. When I talk to people with little experience of quitting or failing (usually younger than me; it takes years to build up a really good portfolio of quitting and failing), they seem like innocent inhabitants of a kinder, gentler country. They have not yet developed the fine art of appreciating absolutely minimal indications of well-being, such as being able to take a deep breath, then another, then going on.

People who quit and who fail are not quitters and failures. We are brave flouters of convention. We are risktakers and survivors. We don't take anything for granted, and we don't accept received wisdom. We ain't afraid of nothin' or "nobody."

And we take your breath away.

*Cellan Jay*
Toronto, Ont.

## A PORTAGE TO MORE UNDERSTANDING

"Go to hell!" he hissed. "I don't want to listen to you, got my own problems. Get lost." I could hardly understand what he was yelling in his jumbled mixture of Quebec French and broken English. But his intentions were clear. He didn't want to talk to me. Nice, helpful guy.

I was travelling in western Quebec on the Dumoine River, which flows into the Ottawa River northeast of Algonquin Park, and had landed my canoe on a small sandy beach. A wood-canvas canoe with some tripping gear indicated that another paddler was already there and I wanted to talk to that person. I hoped to find someone who could give me inside information on the river, interesting tidbits not mentioned on maps and in trip reports: maybe a local fisherman or a trapper who knew all the secret spots that make these places such a delight to explore.

But the young man I encountered on that beach was in a truly foul mood, refusing to listen to me, raving and ranting about that stupid outsider bothering him here in his very own country on his very own river. I tried to explain in my best French that all I wanted was a bit of advice.

Suddenly he stopped yelling, looked at me intensely and said: "So you're not English then?" Apparently he had heard from my Dutch accent that I was not one of those damned born-and-bred English Canadians whose cursed ancestors, almost 250 years ago, had conquered his beloved Quebec on the Plains of Abraham, forever changing the lives of his people.

"No," I said, "not English. I come from Holland. But I'm Canadian, yes, just like you." I obviously shouldn't have said that. He started yelling again.

"I am not one of your rotten Canadians! I am a proud Québécois and I don't want to be insulted by anybody who has no idea at all about what it is to be oppressed in your own country." Obviously something was bothering him.

After a while he calmed down a bit and glumly explained that his temperamental outburst was triggered by my approaching him in that hated English instead of French, the official language of his province. Besides, he was in no mood right now to be nice to anybody because he had just found out that the video camera he was using to record some river locations for a documentary had been badly damaged by humidity. His camera case had leaked and water had destroyed the delicate instrument beyond immediate repair.

There we were. One fervent Quebec separatist who wanted to kick all Canadians out of his land, and one import, a Canadian-by-choice who truly valued his new country. One with a busted camera and one in need of information. There obviously were some problems. It didn't look good.

But maybe because there were only the two of us on that beach, the sky cleared up somehow. He apologized for his outburst; I apologized for speaking English to him. After shaking hands we decided to help each other. He would give me as much information as he could on the river he knew so well, and I would lend him one of my still cameras and some slide film that I had brought along to photograph this exceptional river. At least he would then have some reference pictures of what he might want to film on another trip.

It worked out fine. We travelled as a team for about a week: paddling, portaging, running rapids, swatting black flies, camping, swimming, photographing. And talking! Talking about ourselves, our backgrounds, dreams, love of canoeing, nature, photography, filming, travel, people. We talked about the Canadian Shield, rivers, lakes, fur trade, voyageurs, cultural diversity and many other things that make Canada special.

And we talked at length about the huge problems facing this country: the economic domination by the U.S., the consequences of Quebec separation, the rights of Canada's Native population, our quickly diminishing natural resources. We fully agreed there are no easy answers here; the problems are too deep to be solved by easy answers. There will always be differences.

But at least we sat down together, communicated, developed a dialogue, talked, exchanged ideas, tried to understand conflicting points of view, even started to trust each other. We laughed and yelled and cried and cursed, learning to recognize each other's diverse demands and aspirations, getting a lot closer to appreciating what makes us tick.

In the end, my tripping partner still passionately thought separation could work, although I tried to convince him it might mean the end of both Canada and Quebec.

However, there was one thing we wholeheartedly agreed upon: those politicians in Quebec City and Ottawa should all go on a canoe trip together and solve their problems on the water. They might even develop some mutual respect and a better understanding!

When we finally reached the Ottawa River, each went his own way. He turned east to go back home and I went west upriver to continue my hunt for canoeing photographs. We looked at each other with a new appreciation of our dreams.

"Good luck," I said. "Good luck, my Quebec friend."

"*Bonne chance,*" he grinned. "*Bonne chance, mon ami canadien.*"

Antoni (Toni) Harting
Toronto, Ont.

## RISK TAKING THE HEAT
## TO GET INVOLVED

The morning news tells of a "heat emergency" and a parent being charged with leaving his children unattended, after two little girls had been left in a parked car in sweltering heat. Someone got involved.

The morning paper several months ago told of a small child in another city found dead in an empty apartment.

A tenant was quoted as saying she had often heard the child crying—and wondered. "I should have went up there and checked, but I didn't want to be a snoop. I should have checked on him," she added. "Now I'm wondering if he was alone and crying for help."

Sadly, most people, otherwise responsible, are reluctant to get involved. I can understand that reluctance, for I, too, experienced the dilemma of minding one's own business as against intervening in a dubious rescue mission.

En route to Vancouver Island recently, I was about to exit my car when the cries of "No, Daddy, no!" made me stop, one foot on the concrete deck. I had lagged behind until the other auto passengers had cleared the stairwells. Fearful, I turned my head to the right, then left, then right again as more anguished cries enabled me to zero in on the station wagon immediately behind me in the next lane.

In the gloom of the car deck's interior I could make out a heavy-set man with long, dirty-blond hair, wearing a red-and-white striped rugby shirt. He was seated behind the steering wheel, evidently engaged in an altercation with a small child, whom I only glimpsed in a brief flash. I was aware of a flurry of activity: gesticulating hands, thick shoulders and large, muscled arms flailing about in gestures that appeared ominous, and, intermittently, the wrenching cries of a faceless child.

One minute the untidy blond head would be turned away from me, facing the back seat, the next he seemed to turn his attention to the floor of the car on the passenger side, as though pursuing a moving target.

I continued toward the staircase, hesitant, uneasy, then abruptly turned and headed back to my car, no plan in mind, only "red-alert" flashing in my brain.

The angry scene continued unabated. I could hear the child's cries, see the rage on the blurred face of the father, the arms still flailing wildly. Inwardly trembling, I affected the pose of someone who has forgotten something. I re-entered the car, and pretended to be methodically searching through the glove compartment, meanwhile adjusting the mirror to reflect what was happening in the jeep. The stocky man was unaware of my presence. Although it was not possible to see clearly what was happening, the anger was palpable, even from a distance, and the child's anguish was unmistakable.

Should I get involved? What would I say? Could I pretend I was a social worker, perhaps, instead of just a nosy grandmother butting in on what was probably a child's temper tantrum? I could make a fool of myself. Let it go, said the sensible me—unconvincingly.

A ferry workman walked by. I jumped from the car, motioning him around the corner, out of sight of the wagon. His astonishment at this confrontation gave way to concern. He was not unsympathetic, peering around the corner to observe for himself, but clearly uneasy, doubtless cursing his luck. It was his last shift of the day. "Maybe he's just being a dad," he suggested, weakly, the implication being that this could indeed be an unruly child out of control. "Do you want me to report him?" His reluctance was tangible.

Did I? What real evidence did I have of abuse? Had the father actually hit the child? I thought so. But I wasn't certain. It was a gut feeling, uncorroborated. Supposing I was terribly wrong? What if the child was indeed an out-of-control brat? Had I forgotten what it was like to cope with a temper tantrum? Yet recent newspaper stories told of increasing episodes of child abuse, some of which would not have happened if someone had just noticed. Wasn't I a "someone?"

I struggled with tears of frustration as I pondered the offer of a report. To whom? Instead, I asked the attendant, lamely, if he could instruct the man that passengers were not allowed to remain on the car deck, a cop-out that left me feeling ashamed. It was true—I was as reluctant to get involved as the hapless attendant I had commandeered. But at least an innocuous reminder of ferry rules would get father and child out in the open without my having to intervene.

The attendant appeared to consider this while studying his feet. Then, after another furtive peak around the corner, he reported that the father now appeared to have an arm around the child. Yes, he could see the boy calmly seated in the front seat with his father.

The ferry worker, a kind man, looked relieved. We smiled at each other, self-consciously. All's well that ends well.

We had both played the game, each attempting to shift responsibility to the other. Now we were absolved. We parted then.

I saw the stocky man in the red-and-white shirt in the cafeteria. He and the child were about to leave as I settled in with a pot of tea and a book to while away the time.

The boy looked okay, just your average kid, except for the puffiness around his reddened eyes. I watched as the father carefully gathered up the remains of their meal—

the cardboard container "ferry-pack" kid-food that children like, plastic pie forks, the empty soft-drink containers— and deposited them in the rubbish bin. A tidy man, just being a dad.

I opened my book and carefully concentrated on the words.

All's well that ends well, I told myself.

Was it? I'll never know.

*Pat Gould*
Vancouver, B.C.

## TAKE ME BACK TO BORING NORMAL

The exceptional beauty of normal.

I guess what I miss the most is the average day, the routine, the time when everything was as it was, a kind of sublime normalcy.

While others crave the unexpected, search for thrills and a break from their everyday lives, I want, most of all, the life I had before the illness returned. I want the 9-to-5 life many are so quick to disparage—the common cadences of daily existence most want to escape.

I've had Crohn's disease for 20 years. Now 30 years old, I was diagnosed at the unusually young age of 10. Crohn's sufferers are often plagued by severe abdominal cramps, diarrhea and weight loss, among other things. Drugs or surgery can push patients into remission, sometimes for several years, but it always comes back. When it does return, it sweeps away everything in its path and takes over, its imperious hand wiping away the little and beautiful things that make up our daily lives.

I've spent the past few months in the hospital, a place that is paradoxically no place for the ill. Whatever attempts are made by hospital staff to enliven, or to add warmth to the place, it remains cold, sterile and forbidding. An oversized print of a Monet painting, as soothing as it might be in any other setting, can hardly overcome the sensations of the numerous pin pricks in your arms and buttocks, the tube attached to your wrist feeding nutrients into your body and, above all, the general feeling of malaise that accompanies illness. It seemed out of place, even cruel in a way, in its reminder of the beautiful things on the outside, the things from which you are now so divorced.

Hospitalization forms the starkest break in routine. Holidays, other celebrations and the change of seasons come and go; the normal rhythms of the outside world seem strangely foreign, still vaguely familiar, but somehow distant. The ill inhabit a peculiar, liminal space between the imperatives of their illness—an intractable force that turns them inward—and the quotidian universe outside of themselves.

The only sense of privacy is provided by a thin, often stained and garish-looking curtain pulled around your bed. The sounds of your roommates are clearly audible, you come to quickly know what their problems are, and you guess they know your story, too. Smells, malodorous and pungent, assail the nostrils every day. The smell of feces, urine and blood pervade the halls and your room—there's no escaping it. It seeps into your skin, hair and clothes.

Doctors, nurses and student physicians may walk in at any time, and you feel like a zoo animal as passersby can't resist the temptation to look into your room. If it's a teaching hospital, you'll be asked to play yourself in a peda-gogical demonstration of examining techniques where students will crowd around your bedside, some hanging on every word, others hardly containing their yawns. As for doctors, well, they see you like the cable guy sees you: sometime during the day, can't really tell you when, or if, frankly, they'll come at all. But make sure you're there to meet them.

If there is a normalcy to illness, if there is a day-to-day routine, it consists of blood, drugs and human waste. There are specific times for medications, pain killers and taking blood. Even your "emissions" are carefully measured; the nurse will ask you, for example, if you have "voided" today. Apparently "pee" is not scientific enough.

At the hospital, perhaps more than any other place, there are reminders of our fragility and the inevitability of death, the most violent break with the rhythms of our everyday lives. One roommate has a lawyer visit him so he and his family can finalize his will. Another dies in front of me: another unwanted hospital story.

He was a frail, tired old man, in his late 70s, maybe early 80s, but this wasn't supposed to happen. When the physiotherapist arrived he was eager to go for a walk, and they exchanged a few words as they left the room arm-in-arm. When they returned from their short journey, he sat in his chair, and as far as I can tell, simply, quickly and peacefully wound down. He sat still, his head resting on his chest. Curtains were pulled and I was left with an auditory account of the final moments of his life.

He was unresponsive, the term the medical staff used. They twice called his name. Nothing. A young doctor, who looked as if he may still collect hockey cards, called for a "real stat" and directed nurses to insert an IV. Drugs were pumped into his body as the nurses searched for a pulse. A nurse poked her head behind my curtain to ask how I was doing. "Fine," I lied, shielding my head to cover the tears that came down my cheeks. I thought maybe I'd be tougher than this, perhaps as cool and collected as the voice of Doctor Junior, but what I felt was a sense of panic and an unyielding surge of remorse for this man and his family. Not enough practice witnessing death.

Two days earlier, they had been discussing his release from hospital. Two days earlier, his daughter had spoken with a homecare worker to discuss the arrangements. And now this. "So it goes," Kurt Vonnegut once wrote.

Doctor Junior could have been ordering pizza. His voice was calm, his mind focused, there was no sense in his intonation that a life was hanging in the balance. "Any other suggestions?" he asked. "No? Then I call it."

That was it. My curtain remained closed as they called the "body people."

All I want is a return to the normal, the banal, the pedestrian, the stuff that comprised my every day, that make living, maybe not so exciting, but beautiful in its uneventful routine.

*Michael Dufresne*
Kingston, Ont.

## I LET A SONG GO OUT OF MY HEART. AND GET INTO MY HEAD

Well, there I was, just a walkin' down the street, singing, *"Doo wah diddy, diddy, dum diddy doo."* I looked bad. Felt worse. Definitely not reflecting the upbeat sentiment purveyed by this retro-adolescent beat.

A sleepless night playing butler to my indoor/outdoor cat, while tossing and turning over recent personal and world disasters, had left me cranky and nervous. It wasn't until I raced across a busy intersection and found myself standing on the sidewalk inhaling exhaust fumes from the last bus that could get me to work on time that I noticed this bouncy background music playing over and over in my head.

Trying to pinpoint the precise moment when a song enters my brain cavity and becomes trapped there is a constant source of puzzlement. In this particular case, it had entered a full five nights previous, which I deduced after tracing my steps back to a Friday night TV show my teenaged son had watched in the living room while I washed dishes in the kitchen. A retrospective on songwriters from the early days of rock 'n' roll had included this intellectually bereft, yet catchy, tune from the Sixties. It had lain dormant in my brain's tape recorder until that morning, with the on switch programmed to activate at the most inappropriate moment.

Come to think of it, I always have a song in my head, and usually have no idea how it got there. Sometimes the source is obvious, as when my son was a very young munchkin and sat through his videotape of *The Wizard of Oz* so many times he could lip-synch every line of script and chorus. In those days, I would simply click my heels together three times and head off to work *"Because, because, because, because, becaaauuuse, because of the wonderful things he does."* It was either that or the theme song from *Sesame Street*—a chirpy chorus of children's voices to begin my reluctant trek to the office, where I would greet my co-workers with a psychotic grin on my face. Happy, happy, happy.

I suppose my parents, rest their souls, would be pleased to know their adult daughter greets each day with a song in her heart. What parent wouldn't want that for their child? But, truth be known, it is more of a curse than a blessing, especially in my case, where the incessant background music becomes an unwelcome intrusion that is impossible to shake.

There are times when I think I'm going crazy. We're all familiar with news reports of people who claim to hear voices commanding them to act out in antisocial ways, even to harm their loved ones or join a bizarre religious sect. I sense a connection here, and it scares me. What if I suddenly burst into song in the supermarket checkout line, uncontrollably blurting out the commercial jingle to accompany my cereal purchase? Heads would turn and eyes would roll, as they would if I were to succumb to the urge to sing in the subway, *"I'm singin' in the rain, just singin' in the rain. What a glorious feeling, I'm happy again."* Even if I'm not.

Sometimes I get lucky and the tune only spins around for a few hours before moving on to the next random selection. But, more often than not, the needle gets stuck in the same groove for days on end, subsiding only during sleep and starting up again the minute my eyes open. These are usually tunes of the unwelcome and stubborn variety such as theme songs from family sitcoms, picked up like unwanted fleas in a room, or horrid pop tunes that only very young children or musically challenged adults would listen to by choice.

Like trying to rid oneself of the hiccups, extreme meas-
ures must be taken to flush out particularly bad songs that
threaten my health and drive me to the brink of insanity.
Thus, even though it eats away at my conscience, I have
found the only way to rid myself of one song and move on
to the next is to transfer it into someone else's head. This
can be accomplished by saying to a friend or acquaintance,
"You'll never guess what song I have in my head." Most
people with half a brain do not respond to this statement,
but I press on anyway. Somehow the telling of it helps
diminish its power, like zapping Mario with an electronic
fireball. The torch has been passed and I can move on with
my life.

Still, the point of entry remains a mystery. It could be
something as simple as reading about Elvis's birthday,
attending a school concert or riding in an elevator. Once
the seed has been planted and the germination process
begun, there is no force on earth strong enough to squelch
it from springing up in my psyche when least expected or
wanted.

Apologies are in order. If, in the very near future, you
find yourself tripping down the street on a particularly foul
morning singing, *"Doo wah diddy, diddy, dum diddy doo,"*
feel free to lay the blame on my shoulders.

*Valerie Meadows*
Toronto, Ont.

# FACES

# WHAT IT TAKES
## TO CONSTRUCT A FUTURE

I'm starting to write a proposal for a dramatic television series. Based on my line of work, its working title is *Trades*. It will feature various men on construction sites—iron-workers and crane operators erecting massive steel beams, plumbers installing medical gas piping in hospitals, and the like. There will be lots of action shots, mighty characters heroically posed, wielding wrenches and hammers, and throwing sparks from torches and grinders.

The camaraderie of colleagues in the lunch trailer, greying heads bent together discussing golf games and pension plans. The reward of payday, tradesmen in line at the bank, the evidence of their toil in their dirty overalls, with all the neatly dressed business people giving them a wide berth.

Whoops. I *did* say "dramatic series," not reality television.

The show will never be made, of course. No one would watch it. No matter how vitally important the work done by our hands is, most people stay as far from the process of building as possible.

But I knew that from the start. I remember telling my friends that I was about to begin my apprenticeship as a plumber.

A half-dozen of us were sitting together. Overachievers all, they were completing degrees and going on to grad school. And then there was me. A university dropout, I had drifted through several jobs that were unfulfilling in every sense of the word. After my announcement, after they had finished laughing and wiping their eyes clear of tears, they realized that I was serious.

The truth of the matter is, I had no idea what I was entering into. I only knew that I liked working with my hands and that I had to learn something, some skill that was marketable.

The extent of my knowledge when I started was about the same as most people's, gleaned from peeking through peepholes in the plywood hoarding surrounding construction sites. Everything surprised me. I knew that it was hard work, but I didn't expect to lose 30 pounds. I knew that there must be a fair bit to know about construction, but I was surprised at how broad a field of knowledge was needed just to put in pipes. And I didn't expect the expertise and skill levels of the tradesmen I worked with. Sometimes I thought they were magicians, and considered them to be some of the cleverest people I had ever met.

Apprenticeships take varying lengths of time to complete. In Ontario, a plumbing apprenticeship takes five years of work experience and includes three terms of school at eight weeks each. Union members, such as myself, are also required to take hundreds of hours of night-school classes. At the end, there is a comprehensive, government-administered examination. If your marks are satisfactory, you are awarded a licence to call yourself a plumber. To be good takes more time yet. One foreman I worked for used to say, "It takes five years to do an apprenticeship, and 10 years to be a tradesman." I started my apprenticeship 11 years ago and have been licensed for six years.

So after all this time, do I like my profession? Well, yes and no.

There is a picture on my wall, an illustration of a hospital under construction. I started my training on that hospital and worked with some fine tradesmen who taught me the meaning of craftsmanship. Together, we built that place: from the sump pumps beneath the level of the basement to the vent pipes poking through the roof. It is so very satisfying to be able to see and touch the work of our hands.

But there are other times when I wonder if I made the right choice.

That happens on the frustrating days when nothing goes right, and when I see what some of my friends are doing now. I wonder when I am standing on top of a blast furnace in the middle of February, with nothing between me and a 40-kilometre-an-hour wind off Lake Erie. And I wonder in the idle times between jobs, when my family and I are stretching pennies and wondering when I will work again.

Those are the times when I think I should be trying something else.

But things are starting to change. People are starting to write about us in newspapers, elected officials are talking about us and heads of corporations are starting to ask where the next generation of tradesmen will come. They have finally noticed the grey hair under all those hard hats.

So where will the needed tradesmen come from? I've tried to convince a half-dozen young people who needed to learn some employment skills to apply for an apprenticeship.

Not one has ever done it.

What about immigration? We should encourage newcomers to consider taking up a trade. Many countries in the developed world are facing similar shortages, and most of these countries pay better wages. And every tradesman who retires means one less instructor for apprentices.

But we live in a post-industrial world, don't we, that has left old models of employment behind. Keep telling yourself that as you leave the office building that we built and pick up your kids at the school that we built. Don't give construction workers a second thought as you fill up your car assembled in a plant that we built, from parts made in a factory that we built, with gas from a refinery that we built.

Maybe, as construction workers get more scarce, people will start to notice our contribution and start to value us more.

Hmmm . . . maybe there's a chance that my TV show will get made after all.

David Marcus
Hamilton, Ont.

## WELFARE REFORM AND LITERACY

Would you like to know a deep, dark secret?

I lived on welfare in Ontario for four years. It was quite a shock to go from being a middle-class housewife to a single mom living on welfare.

The fact that I lived on welfare is not something I generally share with others: there was (and still is) a great deal of shame involved in the situation.

Three years ago I was removed from the welfare roll when I went back to the University of Western Ontario to finish my English degree. I graduated on the Dean's list and I am currently enrolled in the Master of Divinity program at Huron University College.

Although things have gone well for me these past three years, I know that at any time my situation could change and I could be on welfare again. As a result, welfare reform is something I take personally. But having lived on welfare is only my second-darkest secret, the first—my greatest shame—is that I have a learning disability (LD).

Thanks to testing, admittedly paid for by the Ontario Student Awards Program (OSAP), I have been identified as a gifted disabled learner (GDL). My verbal acuity is quite high: I am able to take in and process information at a high level, and with the support of UWO's services for students with disabilities, computers, editors, and extra time and effort, I'm an A student.

But you would never know that if you based your opinion of my intelligence on my unassisted handwriting. I have no visual memory of text. I don't know how words look. I cannot unscramble words nor can I pick out the word in a group of words that is spelled wrong if it is phonetically correct. I should not be able to read anything above a Grade 4 level, but my strong verbal skills allow me to read phonetically those words that are not part of my rote vocabulary. When I hear the word in my head I usually know what it is.

It takes me about four times longer than average to read anything above the Grade 6 level.

It is not a perfect system: the more complex the text the longer it takes me to read. I have to keep all the words in my head until they have a meaning I can store. No amount of remedial English will help this condition, as I experienced first hand when I endured four years of "special ed" in grade school. For an LD student, flash cards and spelling drills are not the answer. They need proper testing, which can take up to six hours of gruelling tests with a qualified psychiatrist, and cost upwards of $1,000.

Once identified, sufferers need teachers trained in methods that target the specific problems their LD presents. To cope with my disability, I require a computer set-up that cost thousands of dollars, and it took me years of searching to find the software that works best for me. It's not that LDs can't learn—we are not stupid—we just learn differently and it takes a lot of time and money to make it work.

What you are reading is the sixth or seventh draft of this text. I would be embarrassed to show you the first, as it is poorly organized and any word above my rote memory of a Grade 4 vocabulary is spelled phonetically. In my case this is complicated by the fact that I can't tell the difference between the soft vowels, so even my phonetic spelling is inaccurate. In an unassisted test situation, it looks like I'm illiterate.

Thus, it was with dismay that I read about the latest plans of Ontario's Mike Harris government to reduce the number of people in Ontario dependent on welfare: mandatory testing of recipients for literacy and for drug and alcohol abuse.

I wasn't surprised at how positive it all sounded, if you didn't think about it too hard. Who would object to helping addicts get off drugs or teaching the illiterate?

I was annoyed at the casual suggestion that all welfare recipients are stupid or drug addicts. But I must say, it was my knee-jerk, panic response to the word "literacy" that made me livid.

I began to think about what tests might be used to test for literacy: spelling? grammar? What limits would be set? How literate would you need to be to be spared the remedial English classes? If the test results would need to be better than a Grade 4 result, I might not pass. I thank God I will not be subjected to the government's test for I fear that, my English degree aside, I could be labelled illiterate.

Is the government planning to train those doing the testing to recognize learning disabilities? It has not been my experience that welfare case workers have the time, the resources or the expertise to do these sorts of things properly.

Will the government hire the specialists needed to test those who fail the original test to see if they have an LD?

Is the government willing to provide the level of commitment and support to those people who are in need, to help those who are learning disabled on welfare reach their greatest potential?

I'm afraid that those with learning disabilities will simply be shuffled from program to program until they slip through the cracks. The number of people on welfare will decrease, something we can all be proud of. The government will have been seen to have done something.

I don't know what percentage of people currently on welfare will fail the literacy test nor what percentage of them are learning disabled, but this article is for them.

I have taken the time and the effort to find the words they may not have access to, to let them know my heart goes out to them. I want them to know they are not stupid, lazy or crazy. It is not their fault and they are not alone.

If you have, or even think you may have a learning disability, I would strongly encourage you to find a local support group. Many exist to help those with learning disabilities. If you don't know where to look, you can ask at your local library.

And good luck; you'll need it.

*Loretta Zimmerman*
London, Ont.

## "ON THE LIBERATING ASPECTS OF PORN"

The coffee shop was not very crowded, so I was startled when a woman asked me if she could sit at my table. I looked around at the empty tables and then at her, but in the end I couldn't bring myself to say no. I had an open notebook in front of me and a pencil in hand—surely she would leave me in peace. But no, had she intended to do that, she would have taken an empty table.

"Are you a professor or a mature student?" she asked almost as soon as she sat down.

"Neither," I replied. "I'm not even mature." She liked that and I could have kicked myself for encouraging a conversation. On the other hand, I don't think anything less than turning my back to her would have discouraged her from talking.

"Funny, eh? That's just about what I told them when I went to the Mature Students' Centre. I guess they figure 'mature students' sounds better than 'old students' or 'last chance students.'"

She was a bottle-blond in her forties, with big blue eyes, a wide, uncomplicated smile and a well-rounded but not fat body. She must have been pretty once, in a bimbo sort of way, and still is, in a post-bimbo way. That's the kind of prettiness that requires youth, however; otherwise there's very little there. It's not a look that exudes sophistication or intellectual sharpness, rather more the look of an uninteresting life. At once tough and soft, rather like a country singer. Probably loved a man who didn't deserve it. Having finished this instant analysis, I returned to my notebook.

"So if you're not a professor and not a student, what are you doing here?" she asked me opening a bag of chips. "Want a chip?"

"No, thank you," I replied and suddenly felt very, very snotty.

"Well, sure, why not? I'm a graduate student. An *old* graduate student, which makes me not much different from a Mature Student." And so began my friendship with a woman I'll call Arlene.

We met quite often after that. Sometimes we even went out for dinner. She asked questions with the curiosity of a child and answered them with a child's candour. Reflecting on my early appraisal of her as a woman who had lived an uninteresting life, I couldn't help but find it funny that I had never noticed how terribly dull my own had been. When I said so, she replied, "It's not dull if you've lived it. The trouble with my life," she continued, "is that I never did anything, I didn't really live my own life. Things happened to me, that's all. It's only since I sobered up that I finally started living my own life."

Arlene was working as a waitress in a sleazy strip joint. She had no other job skills. When she was young, she was a stripper, starting as a topless dancer but eventually graduating to the full Monty. Asked if she ever did lap dancing, she said she quit before that became common. But she would have, because the decision would not have been hers. Booze, and eventually cocaine, made the decisions for her. With a little advice from the men in her life.

I thought it would be tough for her, working in a bar while staying off the booze herself. No, she said. She went to an Alcoholics Anonymous meeting every day and has learned to take everything one day at a time. "One day at a time. That's the only way to handle life," she told me. But it was very painful. "It's the girls," she said. "They are so much like I was. They're so young. They drink, they do drugs, they strip. At the end of the week, most of their pay is owed to the guys who bring them drugs. They go to the bathroom, throw up, cry. Then they wash their faces, straighten up, and go outside and do their stuff. It's not staying off the booze I find hard. It's watching them."

A day at a time or not, Arlene found things hard to handle. Her daughter, raised in an environment of booze and drugs and a succession of "friends" her mother brought home, was showing an interest in the very lifestyle her mother had given up.

"I could go on welfare," Arlene told me. She hoped that by getting some education she might get a better job, not a great job but something that would take her out of the bar and still give her a living wage. "But for now, I make more money working at the bar. I want to give Tracy what I didn't have."

I didn't think there was much chance of that, but what could I say? I had no better advice. In fact, advice was the one thing I never offered—until the day came when she asked for something I could handle. She had to write an essay. This assignment was tougher than anything she had ever done, she told me. "Oh yeah, my old job might seem hard to you—but you don't need an education to strip. Just being stoned was enough."

At first, my attempts at teaching her the basics of essay writing came to naught. She found the whole thing just too daunting. Finally I suggested that she go at it just one sentence at a time. It seems I hit the magic formula. One day at a time, one sentence at a time. Now *that* is do-able.

One sentence at a time, she completed her essay, and got a B. We went out to celebrate at a coffee house nearby. Arlene called her daughter to join us but there was no answer. She tried several times and finally cut our celebration short. She went home to wait for Tracy.

I didn't see her again for quite a while. I called her, left messages, but for a long time she didn't return my calls. When at last I reached her, her voice, always raspy but nevertheless animated, didn't have the usual zing to it. She quit school. She quit her job. She applied for welfare. Tracy didn't live at home anymore. She was working as a stripper.

That was the last time I heard from her. My seminar in Women's Studies, on the liberating aspects of porn, lost its appeal.

*Gwen Rivers*
Montreal, Que.

## TWO HEARTS FORGE A STRONG BOND

Richard lives a universe away from New York City. He probably hasn't heard about the devastation that has so rocked our faith in mankind and placed fear in the hearts of just about every young person. And if he has been told about the terrorist attacks in New York and Washington, he will not understand.

He is 20 years old and mentally challenged. He lives a desperate life in Bartica, a small town in Third World Guyana. With a population of about 1,200, Bartica is called the Gateway to the Amazon. How ironic. The title conjures up thoughts of a welcome enclave, a nice place to visit. It is not. It is impoverished and living conditions for the most part are despicable. Richard's family is dreadfully poor. They are squatters.

And Richard is dying. He was born with a hole in his heart that should have been corrected years ago. But he has no money and no access to medical care. Still, he survives.

I first came upon Richard earlier this year while on a medical mission to Guyana with the Ve'ahavta, the Canadian Jewish relief and humanitarian organization, based in Toronto. I was welcomed as part of a team that travelled in late February into the rainforest to river villages that have no doctors, inadequate food, and hut-like housing. Most have no electricity and conditions in the villages are unsanitary. Malaria, typhoid, skin and sexually transmitted diseases are prevalent.

For many, the recent, shocking, almost unfathomable events in the United States have served as a wakeup call. Suddenly, people of my age no longer feel invincible. World events have forced us to question our mortality. I have been questioning mine for much longer.

I recently turned 18. I was born with cystic fibrosis, a debilitating, incurable genetic disease that ultimately clogs the lungs and other organs with heavy mucus. Ultimately the mucus shuts down your ability to breathe. Researchers are making tremendous progress with treatment and I am doing extremely well, but my life expectancy is about 40 years.

Richard's is much shorter. It is a miracle he has survived this long. He will not live much longer and he knows it. For the past couple of years, in questioning my mortality—what my life is about, what my purpose is—I grew anxious to begin, on a much quicker timeline, my life's journey. I felt compelled to experience life outside what was familiar to me. I felt I was running out of time. Many day-to-day activities such as school, and long-term thoughts of notions such as potential careers, seemed trivial. I was not thinking at all long term.

So, I went to Guyana. And I met Richard.

He showed up at one of our first medical clinics and walked directly over to me, perhaps feeling a comfort in my age. His clothes were torn and dirty. He was filthy. I was apprehensive. We had problems communicating. His language skills are not well developed. But his smile and his attitude are infectious and I felt a connection to him.

"I pained," he said, attempting to tell me how ill he felt. I called on one of our doctors, who later told me about Richard's heart problem. The doctor also told me there was little to do to help him.

Before he made his way home that day, Richard and I talked. He lives with his mother, stepfather and sister. He is expected to pull his weight. When walking he stops often to rest. He has problems catching his breath. Still, his abusive stepfather demands every day that he fetch fresh water for the family. Fresh water is hundreds of yards away and he must carry it in large buckets, one in each hand, and climb a steep hill to return to their home. Lack of oxygen often disorients him and he passes out on the trek. As he left our makeshift clinic, I believed I would never see Richard again.

However, upon a recent return trip to Bartica, Richard came looking for me. We had obviously formed a bond. I rejoiced when I saw him. His condition had worsened, but his smile remained bright. I sat with a colleague of mine and talked with Richard. He understands that his prospects are bleak. We talked about dying and he said he was not afraid. He carries a sense of maturity I have not often seen; yet, he exudes innocence. Mentally he is young, but he is definitely an old soul.

So how could we help him, even in a small way. His clothes were tattered. He had had little to eat in days. We asked him what we could do to help. He mentioned to us that in a market in town he had seen a pair of pants that he loved. With his mother's permission, we took Richard to the market. We bought rice and groceries for the family and the pants that Richard coveted. Then we took him home.

I will never see Richard again. As we left him, he stood by the side of the road, waved goodbye and flashed his ever-present smile. It had been a wonderful day for him, perhaps one of the best he had ever had. But I wondered if he knew that he had given me more than I had him.

We have more in common than he could know. And, while Richard has a hole in his heart, he has filled one in mine.

*Jake Labow*
Richmond Hill, Ont.

## WATCH YOUR STEP: THE POWER OF ONE

There's something so spontaneous and incongruous about a person stumbling that our instinctive reaction—even if we don't want to—is to laugh. Perhaps it's funny because it's not planned. Stumbling is something self-conscious urban dwellers avoid.

After all, everything we do is well-considered. The alarm goes off at a certain time, the subway picks us up at an appointed spot and we dutifully check our e-mail in the morning upon arrival at the office. But falling is a rupture in the space-time continuum; it's something that temporarily jars us—and curious onlookers—from the haze of our hermetically sealed lives.

By the fourth or fifth face-plant, however, it was just plain dangerous and I was feeling bad for just sitting there, watching the parade of falling bodies. Something had to be done.

You see, my second-floor office window looks directly onto the giant new Liquor Control Board of Ontario store at Yonge and Davisville in mid-town Toronto.

Last year, I watched as each day a crew of construction workers turned a vacant lot into a metal skeleton and, finally, into a liquor store.

The only problem is the step from sidewalk to store level. Nobody seems to have a problem on the way in, but exiting is hazardous.

I wasn't so concerned about teenagers who were doing face-plants. They bounce back.

But watching seniors and their groceries go hurtling through the air after popping in for a bottle of Chardonnay was simply too much. I had nightmarish visions of twisted ankles and fractured hips, not to mention fresh produce rolling forlornly onto Yonge Street.

So, I strolled across to the LCBO and explained the problem to a clerk.

"I'm not sure if you're aware of this," I said, diplomatically. "But a lot of people, when they come out of the store, are tripping on the step. Some of the falls are quite violent.

I'm not sure if it's your problem or the city's problem, but someone's going to get hurt or someone's going to sue you. Maybe it's as simple as putting up a sign that says, 'Watch your step!'"

"Oh, I don't tell them anything anymore. Nobody listens," said the exasperated woman, with a dismissive wave of her hand toward what I could only assume was management. "Besides, it's the city's problem."

I asked why, when the occasional panhandler stood on the same allegedly municipal step, store employees were out in seconds to shoo them away, but when people were falling and hurting themselves, it was the city's problem.

"Call head office," she said, bemused.

"Uh, okay," I said, incredulous. I turned and walked out, completely vexed, but not discouraged.

When I got back to the office, I put in a call to the head office of the LCBO and explained to someone that the new store was great, but that customers were dropping like flies on their way out and that it was only a matter of time before we would open the newspaper and read about a lawsuit being launched against the LCBO, or the city, or both.

Someone at head office took down the info. I had done my part, but I wasn't optimistic. I thought for sure the bureaucrats at the LCBO would dismiss me as a crank. Or worse, simply ignore my concern.

One morning the following week, there were three men who looked like engineers staring soberly at the step, clipboards in hand and pencils feverishly scribbling.

Then, the week after that, a construction crew of about 15 arrived and, to my surprise, began dismantling the sidewalk in front of the store, jackhammering jagged concrete blocks the size of small asteroids and carrying away the debris in dump trucks.

Then they put in new concrete and raised the sidewalk so it was level with the step. *Voilà*. No more step. No more hazard. No more face-plants.

It took a while to sink in, but it occurred to me that the phone call had actually worked. This was action. The lumbering wheels of democracy had been jolted, however reluctantly, into a slow, but effective, grind.

One phone call, 18 jobs created and zero face-plants. Let's all raise a glass of Chardonnay. You don't even have to watch your step.

*Stephen Knight*
Toronto, Ont.

## A DEATH UNEARTHED

I tried to get drunk that night.

It didn't take, but I really can't fault the wine. I'm relatively certain it had more to do with the day itself. Here on Vancouver Island, when you get a sunny December day, you make the most of it, taking to the woods to hike or bike and recharge for the foggy days of downpour yet to come.

And so we went, my girlfriend and I, into the woods, to loll in the absence of rain and the majesty of trees, to clear some cobwebs by putting some miles beneath our feet.

Out the logging roads, past the last houses, onto the routes frequented by hunters, mushroom pickers and marijuana-grow operators, to that trail that I had seen a couple of times and where I had always wanted to explore a bit more. We had just gotten out of sight of the car, pausing to evaluate the crossing of an overly rain-swollen creek when I saw it. Or her.

There are dark things in this world, events and people and actions that we don't want to consider, don't want to let seep into our world, lest they destroy the fragile precipice upon which our everyday life balances. When confronted with them, it shakes our root assumptions.

Beside the creek, a little further up the bank, lay a swatch of nylon poking out from under a rock: in fact there were a number of rocks and logs and ferns, too many to be arranged in such a manner. We stepped closer and saw, beneath the poorly grouped rocks: pants, then a cotton T-shirt, then blonde hair, a cheek and possibly an ear. "I think that's a body," were not words I was supposed to be saying that day.

To drive out for the police was by far the longest journey of our lives, every imagined scenario a reality, every possible pick-up we passed a suspect. What if the body wasn't there when we got back? Had anyone been reported missing? What if someone had been watching us?

The RCMP officers, both young and not well versed in the byzantine network of logging roads, were efficient and professional although obviously not well seasoned in this type of discovery. They were careful not to make mistakes, at one point going back to the cruiser and bringing out the manual to follow its steps. The four of us, standing beside this picturesque creek, looking at the pile of rocks and the dark green ferns, tried to make some sense of the scene.

It was a positive thing we agreed, someone, somewhere would be able to put some closure on a missing loved one. That may be true and I hoped it to be the case, but it seemed a great deal like lip-service, like the logical protective sides of our brain were throwing up walls in haste in order to save us from ourselves.

The female officer, two months on the job, admitted that it was the first time she had been at a scene with a body: "Me too," I wanted to chime in but didn't. The humour may have worked but the delivery most definitely wouldn't.

Ever since we made the discovery I had been numb and untrusting of my body, the buzzing starting in my knees, travelling up my torso until it became me. Later, in the car, we would rationalize that this was a physiological reaction for both of us, that some endorphin or adrenaline had surged to our brains and dampened our non-essential functions so that our thought might more clearly focus on potential dangers.

They are evidently powerful chemicals for here, later, at 3 a.m. and after a bottle of wine, I still felt my thoughts could saw through wood, that my eyes would burn through the computer monitor.

Inevitably her life is now framed against the fragility of life in general. A month earlier? Two weeks? A week previous? she was walking and talking, thinking about Christmas shopping and starting her morning with a coffee. I feel ashamed for the indignity my fellow humans cause.

I have no idea as to her name, hometown, exact age or anything about her. This is the most difficult aspect to deal with in a Pandora's box of new and raw emotions.

Reality is always such a pale imitation of the worlds we create in our mind. To me she has been a pauper and a princess, a hapless victim of a game gone too far and the manifestation of a great evil.

Eventually I will find out more, but the urgency will be gone, life will fill back the crevices of my mind from which it was so rudely pushed and she will be diminished.

Never forgotten, but diminished in order that there be more room for sunny days. Sleep well.

*News sources say police later identified the body as that of 29-year-old Carla Jannine Slots and confirm she was murdered.*

*Steve Hughes*
Vançouver Island, B.C.

## A LOUSY JOB WITH GREAT BENEFITS

Last year, as I walked down the hall of a brightly coloured office en route to my new desk, I thought to myself, "This job is going to be the one." After five full-time contracts as a student intern and an entry-level position as a graduate, I desperately wanted this job to be "the one." What "the one" meant was simple: a dream job where my talents would be respected, where I'd finally be treated as an adult, and where my career would take off. Not much to ask.

It took me just four months to realize that this job was not "the one." In fact, it was worse than the jobs I'd had in high school. I disliked everything about my new company. From sharing an office with my two bosses, to working on a computer that crashed every hour, to having to miss the Christmas party because I had too much work to do. The job couldn't get any worse. But then it did.

I returned from Christmas holidays to learn that a large corporation had purchased our struggling little company. We were all assured that the new company provided superior financial and benefit packages, not to mention employee incentive programs. The only downside was that very few of us would actually become employees with the new company.

With our jobs as day-to-day, morale sank to an all-time low. We realized that at any moment we could be asked to clean out our desks. The tension in the office was unbearable. Something had to be done to keep our spirits up.

Naturally, our new management wasn't keen on paying for a staff outing, so a few of us decided we needed extracurricular activities to take our minds off the situation. Why not a book club?

I don't know why the prospect of a book club made us all so excited. Maybe it was the idea of seeing our co-workers in a social setting without our bosses around, or because we could try to guess what types of books the person we sat next to read in his or her spare time. Whatever the reason, about 15 people signed up.

The first meeting of our book club took place on a Thursday night in January, right after work. We had chosen the book weeks before and had made reservations at a trendy restaurant close to the office. As we started to trickle in, subtle changes began to take place. We started to smile—that was the first noticeable difference. Then we began laughing and sharing stories that related to the book. The stresses of work were fading with every new opinion of the story. For the first time since joining the company, I could see a real camaraderie forming. Before the night had ended, we had already selected another book and place to meet.

The book club meetings became a monthly ritual. Some months we opted for a potluck dinner at someone's house instead of dining at a restaurant. The day of the week changed too, according to schedules. But, without fail, the first week of every month included a meeting.

Back in the office layoffs, resignations and dismissals became common. We even started taking bets on who would go next. While employee after employee left the company, the book club attendance actually started to increase.

Finally, after months of uncertainty, the little company with the big problems was closed for good. Five employees ended up staying with the new bigger and better corporation, while the rest of us went our separate ways. I had actually resigned a month before, so the official closing didn't cause me much grief. Still, a little voice inside reminded me that if not for that job, I wouldn't have had the book club all these months; the one group in my ever-changing life that stays constant.

The book club is now about friendship. Naturally, we discuss the book and choose a new novel for the next month, but we also get a chance to catch up with one another. How are our new jobs going? Who is moving to a new house? Why isn't so-and-so here? We are each other's psychiatrists, editors, cheerleaders and, most importantly, friends.

These friendships come home with us; we are not merely book club friends. Rarely does a month go by where I don't meet a fellow member for lunch or catch a movie. Not to mention the dozens of e-mails that get traded every week. We still turn to each other when we need some cheering up.

When I think back to my days at the brightly coloured office, I remember the management tirades, the endless meetings that produced no solutions and the constant feeling of insecurity. I wasn't respected on a professional level, management did not treat me like an adult and the job did nothing to help my career.

Still, it did provide benefits far superior to the standard dental and health insurance I thought I'd be getting. It gave me the chance to meet some of the smartest, most resilient people I've ever known. It also gave me motivation to stick with things, even when the situation is unpleasant. While that job may not have been "the one" I'd always wanted, it turned out to be "the one" that I really needed.

*Kristine Gordon*
Brantford, Ont.

## I'VE GOT THE BLUES: I COULDN'T BE HAPPIER

I was stung by the blues long ago. Specifically, my fascination is with the harmonica, or, as it is called when it is used to play the blues, the "harp." It makes me smile, even giggle. And one time it transformed me.

I can play the harp, badly enough to get the dog howling (I suspect she thinks the sounds I make have something to do with my death) and well enough for my son Nick to laugh and for me to appreciate how difficult it is to play at the level of the masters—the African-American pioneers Little Walter Jacobs, Big Walter Horton, James Cotton, Sonny Boy Williamson I and II and, my harp hero, Sonny Terry.

And there is another player, who is certainly up there with Sonny Terry. I saw him perform only once, just for a few minutes, almost two years ago in Toronto. But even with this brief exposure, I knew he had "it." This guy could *really* play.

He was a street person, with the long, matted beard, the hollow eyes and look of hopelessness and homelessness that is too common on the streets of big cities today.

I met him on a blustery, grey Sunday morning in November.

I had just dropped my son Sam off at an appointment in the pretty neighbourhood around Yonge Street and Eglinton Avenue in north Toronto. I had an hour to kill. After puttering around the bookstores, I decided to get some air and sat on some steps in front of a shop that sells organic soaps. The wind was blowing hard and shooting grocery bags and stray newspapers into the air.

And from out of this wind, I heard the most wondrous sound.

There are a lot of ways to play the blues on a harp. Little Walter specialized in a dirty, growly sound indicative of the

Chicago school of blues. Sonny Terry, on the other hand, often went for a country blues flavour, peppered with his famous "whoops." Either way, I think the best blues harp players achieve a surprising sweetness, when the music loses its edge and takes on a playful, joyous feeling.

That's what I heard this time. When I found its source, sitting in front of a Shoppers Drug Mart, I couldn't believe it. Moments before, I had seen him wandering up Yonge, bags in hand. Now, he was blowing that harp like Sonny Terry himself. And the more I listened, the better he got.

I put $10 in his box. He stopped and nodded, with a rather embarrassed smile. "You are fantastic," I said. He nodded again in thanks. I had to say more. "No, I mean it. You really are something."

What I wanted to add was, "What are you doing out *here?*"

Maybe he knew what I was thinking. "I-I-I-I-I-I-I-I-I-I-I ussssssssssed to pppplayyyy the ggggguitttar, but the Pppppppppppparrrrrkkkkinson's . . ." he said. He held up his hands. They were shaking, and it wasn't from the cold wind.

A wave of sadness came over me when he said this. For more than a year, I was frozen on the notion that life is so horribly unfair sometimes. I thought about this man every day. In fact, I didn't play the harp all that time. I couldn't find the joy in it anymore.

But one summer day, the tragedy of his situation gave way to a curiosity about that sweet sound he played. "How did he do that?" I wondered. I tried it. It was hard. "Too hard for me," I thought. Frustrated, I was just about to put my harp away, but I thought of this guy, remembered him sitting on the sidewalk, in the cold, with Parkinson's shaking his body, and how he was *still* playing.

So I gave it another try. And another.

I'm still trying. But his example opened something up in me. I've since found a passion for the harp that I hadn't known. Actually, I've found a new passion for pretty much everything. I've gone deeply into the blues, into learning about the people who invented it and why they invented this music, which is as much a form of emotional therapy as it is a musical genre. "There was a big difference between having the blues and playing the blues," said writer Albert Murray in the PBS series *Jazz*. "Playing the blues was a matter of getting rid of the blues." He's right about that. I know it.

I've even connected with my kids in a new way. I recently got Glenna and Sam to watch (after much pleading) a video of Sonny Terry playing with his partner, guitarist Brownie McGhee, on a Pete Seeger TV program from the 1960s.

"When you listen to rock music today," I told them, "these are two of the guys who invented it." Glenna and Sam are teenagers, so, of course, they rolled their eyes at their old man lecturing them, once again, on the glory of days gone by. But there came a special moment when Sonny was wailing away on *Rock Island Line* and the kids got quiet, their eyes widened and they looked harder at the screen, with a faint, but real, glimmer of "How's he do that?" I'm positive they were stung, too. My heart just soared.

Isn't it something how I have been so profoundly inspired—changed, really—by people who have been so down on their luck—so *oppressed*. The masters of the blues were, well, African-American, the descendants of slaves. Sonny Terry was also blind. Brownie McGhee walked with a pronounced limp, the result of polio in childhood.

My newest hero has Parkinson's disease and played for coins in the cold November wind.

And it's got me thinking that their story wasn't their oppression, or their sadnesses, but what they did in spite of it all. It's clear to me now that the real inspirations in life are often from the people you'd least expect.

I owe these blues people my thanks for taking me deeper, making me think harder. And I owe my Yonge Street harp virtuoso a hell of a lot more than the 10 bucks I gave him.

Now, if I could just find him and tell him that.

*Paul Fraumeni*
Toronto, Ont.

# PLEASE OFFEND ME—
# AND LET ME OFFEND YOU

What would you say if I told you, in all confidence and between the two of us, that I think women are intrinsically inferior to men? That, being of lesser intelligence, they deserve the salary discount they get, and that their role in society should be strictly limited to having kids and cooking supper?

What if I said that it is my personal conviction the Indians of Canada themselves are to blame for their sort, more so than the system they simultaneously abuse and attack? If I told you that I believe that low salaries in developing countries are a necessary condition for our prosperity? Would you listen to me?

It would not help my case, would it, if I added in passing that I am a university professor and that my students are forced to listen to some of my thoughts as part of their degree requirements. You would probably be angered by my remarks, by my cynicism and disregard of the law and other social conventions, and would strongly demand that immediate action be taken, so as to guarantee that no subsequent damage is done.

You would certainly feel much better after action had been taken. You would feel righteous, dizzy perhaps with the quiet satisfaction bestowed on those who have done the correct thing. Yet, you would be wrong. For I am not as bad as you think I am, and perhaps I do not believe any of the things I just wrote. Yet, I am guilty by association. I think dangerously, therefore I must be a dangerous person as well.

Is there a difference?

To some individuals, there is not. Offensive behaviour, our society has decided, should not be tolerated. Violence against women, discrimination based on ethnicity or sexual orientation (among many other forms of abuse of power) have been declared fundamentally incompatible with our ideals, and consequently outlawed. But in the process of correcting some of the ills of our society by decree, we have tended to amalgamate action with thinking and have started putting them at the same level, as though they were the same.

And since many have been deeply offended by remarks made by commentators with whom they disagree, a significant effort has been put into creating non-threatening environments where strong opinions cannot be expressed without fear of being persecuted. Offensive speech (by the listener's standards) is less and less accepted, as we become more intolerant of distasteful ideas. Consequently, thinking and speaking have become perilous: better to shut up than to offend your neighbour, lest you end up prosecuted for something you did not do but merely wrote, something you simply imagined.

Now let me tell you what I really think: I think that in pursuing a noble objective, we have failed. Instead of producing an environment where people could exchange their thoughts, obviously as rich and diverse as their backgrounds and beliefs, we are instead working our way to the operating room equivalent of a public place: sanitized, righteous and sterile in all the splendid meanings of the word.

I am appalled by the regrettable situation we are creating: an environment where the people who think and come up with challenging ideas may well be pushed to censor them so they do not risk offending anybody. The people who do *not* think repeat what they believe is correct without comprehending the consequences of their speech.

It is time, I do believe, to reverse the situation: offending is a necessary part of thinking and thinking is vital for a vibrant democracy.

So, would you please offend me and let me offend you?

Tell me what you think, no matter how outrageous or radical your thoughts. Do not accept what I say without thinking about it, and I will not take your thoughts as self-evident. And perhaps you will persuade me that women's role should be expanded instead of restricted, that First Nations have suffered from systematic discrimination and that it is wrong to base our prosperity on other people's suffering.

For the ills of free speech will be corrected with more free speech, not with less. Perhaps also I will persuade you that being offended is not a good substitute for reasoning.

*Pablo Martin de Holan*
Edmonton, Alta.

## I'M RIGHT ON THE MONEY, HONEY

I've heard that the cashless society is just around the corner. Mind you, I haven't peeked around the corner to check. In technical matters like this, I defer to my betters.

They say that credit and debit cards are making bills and coins irrelevant and we soon won't need them. This is not what the printers of bills and the minters of coins want to hear. The printers and minters, together with anyone else who derives income from their services, could be out of a job. So could the counterfeiters.

If they hope to stay in business, the central banks and the mints are going to have to adopt some creative market-ing. I suggest they adopt it from the post office. Just when everyone thought that courier services and e-mail were going to sideline conventional mail, along came personal-ized postage stamps to keep it going.

Like the Queen, we can all get our pictures on postage stamps. The chief difference is that the Queen doesn't have to pay for the privilege. We commoners do. But once we overcome this hurdle, we can foist our faces on the world. We might even become collectors' items. A happy misprint and we could be right up there with the Inverted Jenny.

Many of us seem willing to pay for personalized stamps. Many more, I suspect, would be willing to pay for personalized currency. Wouldn't you like to see your face on a $5 bill or a $1 coin? No? What about your dog's face? What about a caricature of your boss's face? As you can see, the possibilities are intriguing. Whether out of vanity, vengeance or any of a variety of other motives, if we commit to personalized currency, the cashless society will no longer be around the corner. It won't even be in the neighbourhood.

Bills should be easier to personalize than coins. As the post office does with stamps, the central bank would provide bills with blank areas to which pictures could be affixed. Together with the required fee, you would send in the picture you wished to display and indicate the number and denomination of bills you intended to display it on. The bank would send you duplicates of the picture, each with an adhesive backing, along with the requested bills, and you would stick them together. You would then be ready to put yourself, your dog, your boss or whomever into circulation.

I'm not sure how it would work with coins. That's a technical problem, the kind where I defer to my betters. Let them figure it out.

If you think personalized currency is far-fetched, you should look into the history of money. I did, and discovered that many of the things our forebears settled their accounts with were far more improbable than what I am proposing. In different times and places, they used beads, feathers, rice, salt, seashells, whales' teeth, nails, vodka, oxen and pigs. Compared to those, personalized bills and coins seem downright sensible.

Imagine trying to control inflation when consumers could increase the money supply by plucking a chicken and spending the feathers or by digging for clams and investing the shells.

Imagine trying to discourage counterfeiting when vodka doubled as currency and counterfeiters doubled as bootleggers.

Economists tell us that money is fungible. I don't doubt that it is. But if this poses a problem, we can use a fungicide. They say that according to Gershwin's Law, bad money drives out good. This may be true for some. But not for me. I've got a financial adviser, someone to watch over me. Listen, when I get hold of good money I don't let go of it. They can't take that away from me.

Of course, economics is not an exact science. That's why economists seldom agree on anything. One of the greatest economists of the 20th century was John Maynard Kinsey. Or was it Alfred Keynes? Whoever it was, he formulated the economic law that says in the long run, we are all dead. Then he proved it by dying. This was quite a coup because nearly everyone agreed. The only exceptions were a few economic diehards.

One of the leading economists of the 19th century was Jean-Baptiste Say. He formulated an economic law, too. According to Say's law, supply creates its own demand.

This didn't catch on until it was reformulated in the 20th century. The 20th-century version is if you build it, they will come.

One of the founders of economics was Adam Smith. His claim to fame was an invisible hand. No one ever saw it so I guess the claim was true. Milton Friedman is famous for an invisible foot. No one has seen that either, although some claim to have felt it.

Several other economists are known for their invisible heads. Thomas Malthus thought that the population increases geometrically while the food supply grows arithmetically. Isn't that silly? Every adult knows that the population increases sexually, and even children know that the food supply grows agriculturally. David Ricardo promulgated the iron law of wages. But employers no longer pay their help with iron. They'd rather use feathers. They're lighter. Or seashells. They're prettier.

Karl Marx believed in class conflict and revolution. He said no class can get ahead unless it's revolting. He also believed that under communism the state would wither away. It didn't, although he did.

Malthus, Ricardo and Marx have given economics a bad name. Thanks to them, it's known as the dismal science. I think it's time we cheered it up a little. That's why I'm looking forward to personalized currency.

*Joe Campbell*
Saskatoon, Sask.

## SINGING ALONG WITH MY CONSCIENCE

Her face. It's her face I remember. No, not her face exactly, but how her expression changed. She is in my mind today because of the cold. For some, winter's first snowfall brings warm feelings of the holidays. For me, every first frost brings a memory. Mostly of her face, but partly of the man that I was becoming. There is a moment in everyone's life, I believe, that defines our character. As I walked through the snow, I tried to figure out the exact moment I knew that I had a choice.

I saw her while walking with some friends. She was one of those "special" people. I had seen her before. She couldn't really speak much. Her disability, her "specialness" had closed her mouth but opened her heart. She made a mistake in trust. That day she chose me; she offered me a hug.

With others laughing behind me, I let her touch me. Her arms wrapped around me. I put my arms around her. A second later she knew that I was lifting her purse off her shoulder. A cry of despair left her. She sounded wounded.

Then, firmness set her jaw and she grabbed at the purse. She fell to the ground and slid along the ice. Laughter emboldened me and with one yank I pulled her hard into a snow drift. All I could feel was the adrenaline rushing through my body. All I could hear was blood pounding in my ears.

A gladiator disgusted with unworthy prey, I looked to my friends. Thumbs up? Thumbs down? They now looked at me differently. Was it respect? Fear? I couldn't tell. I looked down and saw her. Really saw her. Past disability, past gender, past fear, I saw her. I saw pure humanity. She was every woman, every man, everyone that I had hurt, could hurt, would hurt. Shifting my gaze from her eyes to my heart, I knew that I was becoming evil.

In the crossroads of a moment, my past and my future intersected. This was now about me. Not about my friends. Not even really about her. It was about what I did next. Time slowed and I heard her struggle, I saw her determination, I felt strength as she shouted perhaps the only word that she could say clearly: "No! Noooo!" Then it happened. I discovered conscience. I discovered a small voice inside me. A voice barely heard but loud enough to drown out the cry of past hurts and the roar of present anger.

Decision made, time resumed its course. I let go of the purse and helped her to her feet. She didn't want to touch me now. This moment was important for her, too. This woman who they said can't learn—did. I had taught her lessons about inhumanity. About mistrust. About violence.

Had I learned? About the world—no. I have always known that the world is hard, cruel even. About me—yes. I hadn't known that I was hard, cruel even.

It's hard to change. As the cold wraps its hands around me, I feel the warmth inside.

It's his face I think of now. No, not his face but the faces of those in the car next to me. Like the memory, the day was clear. Ironically, I had worked on a film that is going to teach people with disabilities how to protect themselves against abuse. One of the guys in the film was named Micky. Mick has Williams Syndrome, a genetic learning disability, and is a pretty awesome guy. He is naturally cool. Like people with Down syndrome, Mick has a unique look. I like it. I like him.

He came to Toronto for a visit and I took him for a joyride in my car. We had the top down and the radio blaring. Mick sang at the top of his lungs into an "air mike" and we were laughing ourselves silly. I was having fun. Downtown, I stopped at a light. I noticed a bunch of kids my age looking at the two of us in my car. Me, looking ready for an audition. Mick singing and rocking in his seat. Me, blond. Him, grey. Me, pretending. Him, real. They looked from him to me.

I looked inwards. Was he still there? The man who would perform violence for an audience of friends. I felt their unease with Mick's joyous abandon. I discovered that the guy inside, the man I became, is someone who likes difference. I reached over and pumped up the volume. Mick glanced at me and laughed as I joined in singing.

It was a political act of defiance. A pledge of allegiance, mine to him. Take him on, take me on. Mock him, mock me.

"Go ahead. Try it," I thought. Again blood pounded in my ears as it took a millennium for the light to change. Again, I heard the "roar of the crowd." The stares. Pointed fingers. Giggles. Each hit with the force of a fist. But we sang, the two of us. Loudly. Gleefully. With the green I hit the pedal. Mick screamed approval as we left them in our dust. It felt great.

When Mick said goodbye, he turned and said, "Thanks, man. Thanks for singing with me. You know, when they were looking." For the first time in years I almost cried. He knew, I realized, about cruelty. Someone else had taught him. I waved to him as he left. I wanted to teach him something else. People can change.

Deeply change.

Perhaps, I think as Mick is leaving, change is the only way to apologize.

I hope I have.

*Michael Soucie*
Toronto, Ont.

## VOLUNTEER TO LISTEN
## WITH YOUR HEART

From 6 to 9 every Tuesday evening I spend time with Gisele, who is dying of cancer of the everything.

Like thousands of Canadians, I'm a volunteer. As many do, I chose to work in palliative care, to spend my time with people who are dying.

There was no logical reason why I chose this difficult and rewarding area, no sudden realization that working with people at the end of their lives was certain to enrich my own life. Instead, it happened in a random kind of way: Chatting with a friend at a dinner party, I learned that the local hospice desperately needed drivers. Impulsively, I volunteered and it went from there.

Hospices, I discovered pretty quickly, are marvellous things. The word "hospice"—from the Latin word for host—was originally used to describe lodgings for travellers. And that's what hospices are today—way stations for travellers on the road leading from birth to death. They're located close to the end of that road, with the goal of making the last part of the journey as serene and caring as possible.

The hospice I work for has several programs. Day Hospice is held several times a week for people who are still well enough to make the trip. They arrive around 10 in the morning and stay for a usually delicious lunch, driven to and fro by volunteers. Other volunteers spend time with them, as do a trained staff of two or three nurses. In surroundings remarkable for their warmth and comfort, visitors play games, paint, do puzzles, have manicures, massages and reflexology treatments or just chat with one another.

There's also a weekly evening session for the "care-givers"—the relatives and friends of the sick—where they receive support and counselling, as well as a chance to share their experiences with others.

And then there's the program that I eventually joined. Hospice staff and outside experts give volunteers 36 hours of training that equip them to visit people in their homes, "patients" who are housebound, with only weeks or months to live. What you learn in these training sessions first and foremost is to listen: To listen to women and men who may want to talk about their imminent deaths, to share their fears, their pain, anger, hopes, beliefs. Often, we were told, the dying find it easier to talk to strangers. Families some-times just can't hear them, because of their own grief, or denial or other complex reasons. So we listen.

Sometimes, we're not asked to do anything other than just be there to allow the caregiver a chance to get a break. And sometimes, the husband, wife, mother, father, sister, brother of the dying person will unload *their* anxieties, anger, fears, hopes, memories.

My first patient was Edna, a wonderful 70-year-old woman with a terrific sense of humour and a mountain of common sense. She didn't really want to talk about death at all. Occasionally she mentioned a sleepless night or a bad attack of nausea from chemo or a frightening feeling of weakness. But mainly she wanted to chat—about her chil-dren and grandchildren, her many trips with her husband or her fascinating childhood in one of Newfoundland's most remote outports. She loved her garden, her family, her books (boy, did she read!), her friends. What she hated was her loss of independence, particularly when it came to keeping her house clean.

"That home support worker," she would grumble, "Clearly her mother didn't teach her about corners." We laughed a lot together, shared recipes and stories about our kids.

When she died, quite suddenly (and not too painfully, thank goodness), I felt deprived. Her loss was my loss, and everybody's loss. I grieved. I missed her, but at the same time was comforted by the fact that I had known her.

My experience with Gail, my second patient, was utterly different. To begin with she was around my age—early 50s—young, at least to me. When I first met her she was able to move around, and we sat in her living room and talked politely. She was very reserved and our conversation stayed on the surface—her work, her daughters, her grand-daughter. But as she became more and more ill, we became closer, and she began to talk more about leaving a life that she had badly wanted to hold onto for longer. She had a great boyfriend, she was worried about her youngest daughter and her future, she was worried about her oldest daughter and her lifestyle. I found it harder to keep my composure and serenity, as the reality of her departure became daily more imminent.

As time went on, though, and she became frailer and less able to talk, we hit on a wonderful pastime for both of us: I began reading to her. We started with *The Joy Luck Club*. "I love this," she told me. "It's just like being a little girl again at bedtime." We then moved on to *Angela's Ashes*, which Gail adored. She wept, as did I, at the sad bits. But forever memorable will be our mutual hilarity at some of the funny episodes. "Stop it, Barbara, stop it," she would say as we both gasped with laughter, "I'm running out of laugh energy."

Gail desperately wanted to stay alive until we finished *Angela's Ashes*. But she didn't, and I feel very sad about that. Her death left me angry in a multitude of different ways and for many different reasons. I couldn't help feeling that she was from life "untimely ripp'd" and that she should have been allowed to hear the end of the story.

So now I'm with Gisele. She's only 50 as well, and she is dying courageously and with a refreshing outspokenness. A healthcare worker by training, Gisele is fascinated by her illness and can discuss its ravages easily and with humour. "I blew up like a balloon last night," she told me once. "That's what happens sometimes when you have tumours on your spine."

Gisele is still determinedly living at home. Her buddies in the hospital unit that she visits regularly give her six weeks— tops. "That's good," she says. "Six more weeks is good."

Her days are devoted to following a rigorous routine: up at 10, pills, bath at 11, chair, one cigarette, pills, lunch, sleep, up at 6, chair, one cigarette, dinner, pills, teeth ("the worst, the most exhausting"), bed. As long as she can keep

this going, she can stay out of her final lodging, the palliative care centre.

I'm now reading to Gisele as well. A dreadful John
Grisham novel where murders abound and the defence
lawyer drinks like a fish. It's good stuff and we're both
enjoying it. I'll miss Gisele terribly when she's gone.

*Gisele died shortly after this article was written.*

*Barbara Campbell*
Ottawa, Ont.

## BRINGING THE REFUGEES HOME

Life will never be the same again.

I began my first tour huddled intimately with 16 visitors
in a musty canvas tent, raindrops drumming lightly overhead. I spoke of the fear and insecurity I felt on the
morning of Sept. 11, wondering what would happen next.
Wondering, would my home be the next target? I felt as
though I was back in the field with Médecins Sans
Frontières (MSF), as though the world I had known abroad
had come home.

My experiences of war have lingered like dreams in
faraway places; they have always been difficult to bring
home. The New York terrorist attacks brought back my

feelings of fear. But it was my work in a refugee camp in Ottawa, a camp complete with tents, water bladders, medical centres and a cholera quarantine area, that finally allowed me to give voice to these experiences.

This simulation refugee camp, designed and presented for public awareness by MSF, generated energy even without refugees, even without the dream-shattering noises and stomach-turning odours of thousands of fleeing people.

MSF doctors, nurses and logisticians served as guides amidst the tents, handmade toys and latrines. They shared stories of refugees from around the world. And it was these true stories that brought the camp to life. I worked as one of these guides.

"As a refugee," I explained to the huddled visitors in the canvas tent, "you would have felt a disturbing tension prior to being forced to flee your home. But you would have lived with this tension for weeks, months, maybe even years. Then suddenly the tension would have escalated: your father murdered, your uncle disappeared or news arrived that you or your family had been targeted for elimination. Then, you would have had to gather your family and leave; leave your job, your friends, your extended family and your cultural context."

Leaving home is never easy. For the world's 35 million internally displaced persons and refugees, all facets of life change dramatically, usually permanently. I have never met a refugee who has stopped dreaming of returning home.

Several of my patients, students and medical colleagues were among the visitors that I guided through the camp. I saw the shock on their faces as I told of the 200 to 300 patients a day doctors would treat at the medical tent. I saw tears in their eyes as we talked about the stories of injustice, starvation and death. And I saw soft smiles emerge as we talked of successfully treated children and camp soccer matches. I felt proud to see them at the camp. Their courage to hear the stories and learn of the difficult conditions felt like supportive testimony for my refugee friends.

One MSF guide, a refugee himself, spoke of his work as a volunteer translator in a Kosovar refugee camp: "As an old man told me his horrific story I started to cry. I cried again as I translated the story to an American psychologist, and then she also started to cry. Soon the old man was comforting us. 'It's okay,' he said, 'it will be okay.'"

Through my work, I have come to see refugees: engineers, doctors, teachers, mothers and children, simply as members of my extended community. And I have come to see world conflicts through their struggles rather than CNN news updates. But it has never been easy to share their stories, stories that are often steeped in fear, anger and sadness. Such tragic tales threaten our personal world view and often breed fear and indiscriminate hatred. It takes courage to remain open to these realities, particularly in a climate of fear and insecurity.

No, life will never be the same again. The mock camp transported me back to the field and allowed me to breathe life into refugee stories. Being there allowed me to create a small sanctuary for the harsh reality of refugees. It felt good to know my Canadian community heard the stories and, in so doing, acknowledged some of our world's most difficult struggles.

My time at the camp left me inspired and ultimately allowed me to feel more at home in our uncertain times.

*Kevin Pottie*
Ottawa, Ont.

# PLACES

## DON'T YOU GLOWER, TAKE A SHOWER

Think quickly, please.

Three weeks ago you escaped from a POW camp somewhere in the steaming remoteness of a jungle and you are
now bloody and ragged and filthy, and lice are nipping at
your armpits while festering leeches cling to your inner
thighs, and you are skeletal because you've had only
coconut husks and water rats to sustain yourself, and on
lucky days the odd bit of raw monkey tail.

But now here comes a helicopter. You are being rescued.
You can hardly believe the crew are not just another malar-
ial hallucination, but then they give you corn syrup and a
bottle of chilled orange juice and you know that it's all real.
They convey you to a gleaming hospital.

Now the question, and it is a very significant one, that I
put to you in this situation is: What is the very first thing
you *crave* to do?

I will tell you the answer.

Do not say you want a telephone. Nonsense; you do not.
Don't let's pretend that sex is uppermost in your mind. A

226

fried steak with onions perhaps? No. Rubbish. Nor is it a
big hug from your long-lost spouse, no matter how much
you may pretend that it is.

There is something else that comes first: this is the
truthful answer.

What you want, what you crave, what you *must have*, is
an infinitely long, endlessly indulgent, rakingly hot, deli-
ciously sloppy, steam-baking, pleasantly hissing, musically
tinkling, mulchily soaping, tingle-blasting shower. Oh God
yes—a shower shower shower.

I raise this rather extreme example purely as an imagi-
native means of proving a point: that the shower—its
conception, invention and ultimate mass-production—
represents almost the very apex of human creative achievement. Showering is the best part of modern life. It makes all
of the nastiness wrought by technological progress somehow
worthwhile. It cancels out cancer-causing pollution, urban
sprawl, bureaucracies, spy-cameras, industrial-scale warfare,
even the proliferation of midnight infomercials. It is one of
only two benefits I can think of—the other being medical
advances—that make our civilization bearable. Without
them, we'd all be better off remaining in our natural states,
free and naked as happy children amid pristine nature, like
those natives of the upper Amazon who still hunt with
blow darts.

For the shower is not merely a triumph of hygiene and
luxury but of social justice as well: the shower is democratic. I would imagine they've been built in their hundreds

of millions all over the globe. The shower is sensuous pleasure for the masses; while it may be a commonplace, its delights remain of the rarest variety—what else can one possibly compare with the sensations a shower visits roamingly against the whole of one's bare flesh? It is joy for all the senses: steam and suds-perfume for the nostrils, hot rivulets for the tongue, motion for the eyes and rhythm for the ears, and touch, of course, soft needles of sublime contact. The caress of a shower is located in that most rarefied zone where pleasure only just begins to tip over into almost-pain, where heat almost but not quite burns, where the needles sting without quite piercing . . . all of this and it cleans the body too!

This is why a shower is the first thing you will crave after the jungle.

And then, too, the device also has an inner dimension. A shower constitutes an immaculate tile-lined world apart. One sings out in any key and choirs of angels return in echo. Showers provoke creativity. I get all of my best ideas in the shower. I thought of writing about showers in the shower.

The more one considers the shower, the more remarkable does it loom in one's estimation. They massage you, showers. They console and comfort. They are like psychological transportation units—like the teleporters in *Star Trek* episodes—into which you step as one type of person and emerge as another, refreshed, perfumed, invigorated-yet-relaxed. Your blood glows after a shower.

In the shower one is subsumed within a charming sense of freedom despite, or perhaps because of, being cosseted in a private rectangle, a pocket out of the real world: one is free to bellow or to scrub one's genitals, to hop or spin as you please. Utter liberty. Your hairs are stroked. Your shoulders kneaded. Warm tendrils trace your length like fingertips. There is a soothing that sinks into the very marrows and . . .

Well, I think I've done more than just exult the overlooked importance of showers in modern civilization. I believe I have over-convinced myself—I'll now propose a cult of shower worship. It's the logical next step: from the personal to the communal. We need to teach young people respect for their showers. We must make it a ritual practice to have a satisfying shower before making any important decisions. The mind is cleansed as well as the body. A shower constitutes a superior form of meditation. Even of prayer. A soap-on-a-rope would, I think, serve excellently as a ceremonial chain for our priesthood. A nozzle mounted on a sink as our sacred altar. It makes wonderful sense. Yes. Definitely.

Now all that's wanting is the right action plan for promoting my shower cult. I need some creative ideas. I think I had better just pop under the old showerhead, just for a quick sprinkling moment or two.

*Kenneth Bonert*
Thornhill, Ont.

## MAKIN' A LIST, AND ANOTHER . . .

There are things I do, things I should have done but didn't, things I shouldn't have done, but did, and things I have thought of doing but haven't got around to.

Most of these "should dos," "have dones," "didn't dos," "dids" and "thought abouts," I have written down some-where—on pieces of paper, backs of books, napkins, cigarette packs, even on the occasional wall. I find them between the pages of a novel, in coat pockets, between the seats in my car, under furniture, on bits of scrap in my clutter drawer.

I'm talking about my "to do" lists. There's the basic and universal Shopping List: grocery, hardware, drug store, clothing, housewares, liquor. I have made a thousand of these lists, even though, I have to confess, most of them don't make it to the store with me. So I end up going from memory most of the time. Problem is, I don't always remember the shopping list I just wrote, but an earlier version. I have had up to four dozen eggs in my fridge at one time, which meant a week of cholesterol overload just to use them up. I now add "remember shopping list" to my list—but it still doesn't always work.

And then there's Christmas. I am still in the early stages of composing my Christmas gift list—after all, it's only the end of November. My sister, damn her organized soul, finished her Christmas shopping in July and her parcel will arrive, as always, with three weeks to spare.

My deadline is Dec. 10 to have everything wrapped and delivered to Canada Post in order for the gifts to be at their destinations by Dec. 25. That's gifts for 10 nieces and nephews, ranging in age from 4 to 12, all located west of the Saskatchewan border. Every year, with only four shopping days left 'til Christmas, I am packing up my gift parcel for shipment by UPS at a price that surpasses the total cost of the contents.

This year looks like it will be the same. So I will again add "stop procrastinating" to my "things I have to improve" list.

Then there are the resolutions—New Year's, birthday or any occasion where you suddenly become aware of all those personal refinements you need to have completed before you die.

These come in two categories: the achievable and the wishful thinking. Over the years, my list of mundane, but attainable goals have included: quit smoking (have done), go to fitness classes with some regularity (am doing), attempt to keep my equilibrium when I am confronted by one of my kids in an uncompromising mood (doing somewhat).

I have also added these to my "looks like I'll be able to do this" list:

Resist all temptation to revert to old self—no more occasional cigarettes at parties.

Drink less wine (cultivates urge for cigarettes).

Take a trip that involves crossing the ocean (any ocean).

Lose 20 pounds prior to trip.

That brings me to my ultimate "you just never know what could happen" list. I have to concede that there are a few aspirations that really should be crossed off this list: I will probably never marry Monkees bassist Peter Tork or Paul McCartney. There was that slight chance with Paul after Linda died, but he had to go and fall in love with a one-legged 31-year-old (far too young for him, in my opinion). And I'm a little old to become a famous Olympic athlete, or a glamorous movie star, or a world-renowned foreign TV correspondent. Although I still could have a chance at 60 *Minutes*. After all, Mike Wallace is well over 70. My dream of becoming a Victoria's Secret model is also out—at least until they come out with the Victoria's Ancient Secret catalogue.

But I'm not discouraged. I just keep updating the list:

Become a mature femme fatale and leave a trail of broken-hearted men—all under the age of 35. Their biggest attribute will definitely not be their brains.

Or, I could develop my spiritual side—take meditation classes, become a Buddhist nun, move to a monastery in Cape Breton, become the subject of an Oscar-nominated National Film Board documentary (request to sit beside Pierce Brosnan for the presentation).

Or, write trashy, gothic horror novels and be promoted as the next Anne Rice—make scads of money, start to dress funny.

Or, move to a small town, become known as Ma Simpson, the crusty and eccentric editor of the local newspaper—develop a national following for my no-nonsense "I don't give a damn what you think" opinions.

Or, get a weekly spot as a political panelist on coast-to-coast CBC radio show, with the occasional TV appearance thrown in—drop dead, on air, at age 96.

What's the likelihood of my doing any of these things? Well, I have them written down on a list, so I'm at least part way there.

*Diana Simpson*
Mississauga, Ont.

## A RESPONSIBILITY
## WE SHOULDN'T REFUSE

I wasn't thinking about *The Little Prince* when I ran into Bruce Thomson one day last winter. He told me his plan was to leave our neighbourhood and return to his home and native land. On this particular day, he was recruiting vigorously and asked me to take over emptying bins of garbage along a well-used footpath. "It won't take long, takes me about half-an-hour. It's actually quite fun, good opportunity to work off your anger . . ."

Bruce is from New Zealand and a more zealous New Zealander would be hard to find. During his stint as president of our Toronto neighbourhood called Ashdale Village, he, among others, inspired and gently bullied us to take charge and create a cohesive little community. We've planted gardens, had parties, bought and sold things to each other, collected garbage, liaised with the police on community crime issues and talked with local businesses to improve the village.

One of Bruce's self-assigned tasks was to collect garbage along a tract of land that falls into nobody's jurisdiction. It is apparently owned by CN Rail but, as Bruce explained to me, they seldom deal with the garbage because, as they see it, the garbage was not put there by CN patrons. The city is similarly flummoxed because it is well out of reach of the regular garbage run.

It bears witness to Bruce's charm and persuasiveness that several months ago I started my new job and found myself donning leather gloves, digging out bags containing rotting, stinking contents and cursing like a neighbour I once had.

I empty three handmade garbage containers and two standard, wire-mesh ones. I pull out the bags I placed there the previous week and then haul them up or down steps to the front of a house so the city can easily pick them up with household waste.

During the first few weeks that I was emptying the bins, I began noticing the garbage contents. The vast

majority falls into three categories: bagged dog excre-
ment, junk-food wrappers (tins, paper cups, potato chip
bags and candy wrappers) and incorrectly placed bags of
slimy household garbage. I mentioned the content to my
spouse and his astute response was: "The dog [excrement]
is the most nutritious thing in there—at least for the
Earth."

One week I corralled my nine-year-old son into helping.
I marvelled at his enjoyment of the task. The extra-large
garbage bags became parachutes and I was treated to
frequent "Hey, mom, look at this!" as he jumped down steps
holding the bag high over his head. Other times, he
became the green slime monster and enclosed himself fully
in the bag and pretended to push his way out.

The week after I took my son along, we were using the
pathway and I said to him as we approached a bin, "I wonder
how the garbage is doing?" He answered, "Yeah. Is there
much in there?" The tinge of concern my son expressed
touched me and I realized I was—as odd as it seems—developing a relationship with the bins and their contents.

As intimacy grew, so did my anger. There appears to be
a shared credo among path walkers: If the green garbage bag
falls into the bin, don't fix it, heap garbage on top. This
behaviour means that by mid-week, a hideous mess of
mixed junk must be extracted manually from the bins if
they are to be emptied.

One week as I walked the line, I began noticing the
range of flowers and greenery that springs out through

the wire fence that separates the railway from the path. It struck me that I don't even know the names of any of these plants, which I walk past each week.

I am, however, getting to know my neighbours. One woman greeted me early in my dumping days and after saying thanks, followed up with a harangue about the low-class people that live hereabouts and refuse to take care of their places. I responded with the useful, and non-committal, "Hmmm . . ." sound which has saved me from many arguments.

Another day, I ran into an elderly fellow walking his dog. We talked, and now I see him frequently at approximately the same place and time. Recently, I met Mohammed. He accompanied me on my walk and we managed to get the job done in record time. He also gave me a brief cultural education on language groups in India and Pakistan.

As the weather got warmer, the job became less bearable. Maggots and increased stink greeted me at the beginning of July. More neighbours appear to be using the bins for household waste and things they don't know what to do with. I moved a large bag of gravel last week. I've decided I need a lightweight wheelbarrow and need to put some signs up that explain the purpose of the bins.

But the thing I'm realizing about garbage is that we don't want to know too much about it. And similar to a human being we don't yet know, we feel little obligation to it. Garbage does not relate to us. Generally, we don't even see it.

I was thinking about my son's tone of voice when he asked about the bins. It was the voice of attachment. I remembered reading Antoine de Saint-Exupéry's *The Little Prince* in high school and was sure he had more to say on the subject: Attachment to something comes with tending it, not the other way around.

The thing is, tending these bins means I'm tending the neighbourhood and tending others. So, tending is an exponential process that yields attachment. I now know far more people and animals in my neighbourhood (raccoons particularly) and I am familiar with more plant life. I feel more embedded in my community.

I am, however, left with a question: At what point does the visceral unpleasantness of bad smells and hard work outweigh the pleasantness of attachment, or the curiosity about what will happen next week?

*Carol Watson*
Toronto, Ont.

## THE VIEW FROM RUGGED COVE

Rugged Cove, a fishing village of about 200 people, is on the south shore of Nova Scotia, near Lunenburg. It is a very beautiful place. We live here now.

On either side of the cove, protecting the little harbour, are high cliffs exposed to the wild North Atlantic. There's a lighthouse up there. It's a working lighthouse, but is unmanned now. Once there was a lighthouse keeper. A modest plaque records the name of every keeper the lighthouse ever had, all nine of them, beginning with Captain John Watson in 1820 and ending with James Smith who retired in 1960 when the government in Ottawa decided that machinery could easily replace a man.

The harbour has a government wharf where the fishing boats tie up. The fishermen go out just about every day of the year, even if it's very cold or stormy. A memorial in front of the village church records the names of local men who have been lost at sea. There are many names. "Lost in the arms of the Lord," says the inscription.

The houses of Rugged Cove are clustered around the harbour. Ours is one of them. The houses are picturesque, of many colours and seem artfully arranged, as if in preparation for a painting. Most are quite old—we live in one of the oldest, built in 1840 by the village bootmaker. There are three or four modern homes in the village, but they fit in just fine.

The family names in Rugged Cove haven't changed much over the years. The Smileys, Whynots, Conrads, Clattenburgs, Hatts—they're all still here. If you look at a photograph of the town taken a century ago, and imagine a few cars, well, it doesn't look all that different from today.

Of course, there are a few people who've "come from away" as they say in these parts. There's the Famous Writer from New York who arrives in June for the summer. And there's us. We came from Toronto last year. When we were renovating the bootmaker's house, the locals referred to us as "the foreign developers."

I think it was the refrigerator that got us off on the wrong foot, that encouraged the "foreign developer" thing. The refrigerator in question is a Sub-Zero—big, shiny, new, heavy, the price of a good secondhand car. It was shipped from Toronto. We weren't in Rugged Cove when it arrived—when they took it off the truck and, with a lot of trouble, got it into the bootmaker's house. But we heard later about how the whole thing had gone.

They had to take it around the back of the house, across the new cedar deck with the ornamental railings, through the new French doors (the only doors in the house wide enough to take a Sub-Zero), across the newly polished oak floors in the living room, and into the new kitchen with the granite countertops.

It took the better part of an hour to get that refrigerator into the house. Of course, dealing with comments and advice offered by the small crowd that gathered to watch may have slowed things up a bit.

"Have to take it round the back, through them fancy new doors," said Teddy Eisenhauer at an early point in the proceedings. "That's some fridge you got yourself there." Teddy has been the village handyman for 40 years, and he didn't like it when someone else installed the French doors.

"You're gonna scratch them floors that were just polished," said Billy Munro, who was a fisherman until two years ago when he fell off the roof of his house (he was fixing the chimney at the time) and hurt his back.

People in the village still talk about Refrigerator Day.

Mid-afternoon, here in Rugged Cove, we look out our living room window and watch the fishing boats come back to the wharf. Crowds of gulls follow the boats into the harbour. The fishermen (only the CBC says "fishers") have been out at sea since about six o'clock in the morning. In the winter, in the early morning darkness, you watch the boats leave the cove by following their lights.

Most of the fish they bring back are sold to a small packing plant next to the wharf. It's not easy to get a good restaurant meal on the south shore of Nova Scotia. There just isn't much demand for eating out. You're better off to buy a fish from the packing plant—maybe a 10- or 12-pound halibut—and, in season, fresh vegetables from a roadside stand, and cook at home.

Visitors from Toronto like to take back a fresh fish from the Rugged Cove packing plant. A Rugged Cove fish in Rosedale is part souvenir, part conversation piece, like folk art although less durable. The guy in the plant packs it nicely for you, and it's a good feeling knowing that the fish is in your suitcase when you check in at Halifax Airport, although you'd better hope they don't lose your luggage.

A year ago, in my office high above Bay Street, if I looked out of the window in the late afternoon, I saw cars on the Gardiner Expressway heading west, going home to Etobicoke, Mississauga and Oakville. In the morning, the cars stream out of the west, bringing people downtown to work: in the dark winter mornings, already at my desk, I watched them come by following their headlights.

*Philip Slayton*
Rugged Cove (aka Port Medway), N.S.

## GARDENERS WELCOME
## THE FIRST DAY OF SPRING, 2001

My mother was shocked to hear about my new plot. She hadn't even considered one for herself. I explained that Gramma had me thinking about it and went on to describe the 3-foot by 12-foot area. My mother was unusually quiet. "I thought you were going to get a house first," she said.

I went on to describe my stake, "It's only four blocks from our apartment, entirely organic with composting and ample parking nearby. We can go to the garden every day."

After a pause she said, "Ohhh, I see."

Growing things was not natural to me. As an urban dweller, my experience with gardens was limited to purchasing fruit and flowers at the local grocery. Sometimes, I even bought live geraniums for the window box. By dropping the flowers directly into the empty box, plastic containers and all, I could quickly replace the dead ones before the next dinner party.

Besides, who had time to garden? My adult life was devoted to a busy career, then a husband and now a baby. Yet one sunny day, pushing the stroller down a side street, I came upon an oasis.

In the corner of a large parking lot, a patch of lawn was filled with rows of raised garden beds. The "welcome" sign announced it as a community garden, with both individual plots and volunteer gardens to provide fresh vegetables for the community centre.

Still on the high of motherhood, or sleepless nights, I applied for my own bit of Earth.

There was one plot left. It may have been the smallest box in the garden, but to me it was ripe with possibilities. After buying too many books and seed packets (so much for cost savings), I was soon overwhelmed.

The instructions were specifying finely sifted compost, vermicu-something-or-other, sowing so many seeds in a centimetre of soil, transplanting, hardening-off gradually, cold frames, trellising, thinning. None of it made sense to me. I tucked away the books, ignored the package directions and simply dropped seeds into the soil.

Weeks passed. Miracles happened. Just like the baby created from one pleasant afternoon, the seeds sprouted and grew into a lush, green jungle.

Each visit was an adventure. The frail tomato transplant soon crowded out the whole east end of the plot, stifling the basil and marigolds.

Pumpkin vines invaded the edible pod peas, which in return wrapped dainty tendrils around the prickly vines and used them as a step-stool. We watched a mystery plant grow into a Savoy cabbage.

When the zucchini began to blossom, I excitedly called my grandmother. My jubilation turned to confusion when she first asked after the baby and then whether I was pollinating myself. I explained that one baby was enough for me at this point.

My grandmother proceeded to tell me about the birds and the bees.

"If you don't have many bees, you'll have to help the male pollinate the female flowers."

What? Flowers have gender? No one ever told me that. Even more embarrassing, I didn't know how to tell the difference.

"Uh, Gramma, how can you tell which is which?" She paused for a moment. It suddenly occurred to me that perhaps the question was not appropriate for my modest grandmother. "Well, you know what a male looks like," she ventured. We both burst into laughter, the kind of spontaneous, embarrassed hee-hawing that brings tears to the eyes, an ache to the stomach and pretty much ends the conversation. It hasn't been discussed since.

A later inspection showed that yes, male and female zucchini flowers were different. A healthy gang of bees did their work and spared me the cotton swab procedure. It was a prolific harvest and anyone who stopped by to admire the community garden ended up walking away with a fresh, organic zucchini.

The garden itself taught me more important lessons, like the sheer abundance of the universe as tiny seed-specks bloomed into large crops of cabbage, carrots, lettuce and radishes.

I admired the resilience of nature as the garden survived the onslaught of well-intentioned sprinkling by my toddler—and the droughts in between.

Then there was the quiet determination of the vegetables. Unable to complain about inept supervision, poor growing conditions or lack of opportunity, all they could do was focus on their potential. They grew beautifully.

I hope my daughter will learn some of these lessons earlier than I did. But like parenting, the lessons may not sink in until she has her own responsibilities. In the meantime, I take particular comfort watching the plump vegetables develop after the brilliant flowers of youth dry up.

My professional career has been put on a back burner and the biggest parts of my life taken up with family and garden.

It's difficult to put aside the many years of work and study, not to mention the clean office, uninterrupted adult conversations and lunch breaks.

Yet now I am learning the truly important lessons in life.

As Voltaire wrote: "We must cultivate our garden."

*D.S. Abercrombie*
Victoria, B.C.

## A GIRL, A GULL
## AND ORNITHOLOGICAL TRUTH

There is no such thing as a seagull. Most people don't believe me when I tell them this, but it's true. If you look in bird books, you will find that there are all sorts of gulls, such as Glaucous gulls or ivory gulls, but no Sea gulls. I've always had a bit of a problem with letting people call schoolyard gulls seagulls, so in primary school I became a bit of a nag to all my classmates who used the erroneous term. I think I got some of them to just call them gulls, but not many. I don't mind poetic licence, but in Toronto they are usually Ring-billed gulls. But how did the misnaming of gulls become my *cause célèbre?*

My parents are bird watchers. They take my brother and me out of school for a week every year in May so that we can go birdwatching at Point Pelee, Ont. Point Pelee is the southernmost point of Canada, jutting out into Lake Erie, and it is a prime stop-off point for migrating birds. The spring migration is at its peak during May, around Mother's Day, when thousands of birds pass through the park. Whenever my parents tell anyone that they are taking my brother and me out of school to watch birds, their listeners believe that this is a valuable experience for us. Family bonding and appreciation of nature are often the reasons cited by others for why going birding is more important than a week of school.

My parents don't mention that we get up around 6 in the morning and walk for most of the day. But my brother and I know what to expect at Point Pelee and when talking about it at school, there are often friends who are envious of our missing school and classmates who mock our interest in birds, even though they have never been birding themselves. They are the sort of kids who used to insist on saying "seagull" whenever I was around to see how many times I would correct them before giving up in frustration.

At Point Pelee, there are many people we see every year, year after year, and only at Pelee. I have been going there since I was two months old, so these people have known me all my life. Although they see me annually, they insist on comparing my present size with my baby size. Luckily, my grandmother instituted a rule that every time someone says "My how you've grown!" (or an equivalent, to my brother or me) my parents have to pay us $0.25. We usually get at least $3 in a week.

The people who come to Point Pelee are amazing. Their eccentricities are very amusing, especially to those of us who don't really care about the name of that little brown bird that just hid in the bush. One of my parents' friends always carries a dictaphone with him, and documents his whole experience with it, mumbling along the path: who he saw, what he saw and any other anecdotes. The theory is that when he gets back home he will transcribe the tapes, but so far, he tells us, he only has stacks of tapes.

Then there is the man who used to be a ranger at Algonquin Park, who will explain the field markings of a rare shorebird to you at length while you look at it, but once satisfied that you have seen it, will rush off to where another rare bird has reportedly been seen. He's like all "twitchers," a term given to birders who won't stay in the same place for more than a few minutes before rushing after the latest rumour.

There is a couple we know who named their daughter Kestrel. My brother is consequently very glad that he avoided being called Peregrine, which my parents did seriously consider.

Every morning we take the tram from the visitors' centre to the tip of the point. The gulls congregate there in the morning. The density of other birds is supposed to be higher there in the morning because that's where they first hit land after flying over the lake. I'm not sure if it is true that the birds in the morning are best, but by now it's a tradition and you have to have some sort of routine for the morning. On the way to the tip, everyone discusses things like yesterday's best bird or famous birds of the past. However, the most entertaining event of last year happened one morning when we were on the tram with a bunch of elderly men. It was like being part of the scene in *The Music Man* when the salesmen are discussing the man who "*doesn't know the territory*" while riding the train. One of them was complaining about all the mosquitoes when another started:

"Yes, well down at Rondeau there are ticks and there are chiggers. Don't ever camp at Rondeau. You gotta sit on the picnic tables to stay away from the chiggers, (yes, there are chiggers)."

My mom and I got off at the tip, laughing.

But it's not all fun. On a good day, you're on your feet from 7 a.m. until 10 p.m., but you see a lot of birds. On a bad day, you're on your feet from 7 in the morning until 9 at night in the rain (or wind or Scotch mist) and the cold, with no birds and only a wet lunch to look forward to. There's a saying—when there are no birds there's always lunch.

I'm not a morning person, and by the end of the day my knees and legs hurt. Last year, especially, there were a lot of mosquitoes, rain for about four of seven days and no birds. Rain with birds is pardonable, but rain without birds is unforgivable. Yet in a strange way I enjoy birding. A streak of red is very uplifting on a grey day. I enjoy being able to identify the birds at our backyard feeder.

And I am proud to know that there is no such thing as a seagull.

Georgia Carley
Toronto, Ont.

## WHAT I DIDN'T DO AT SUMMER CAMP

One fine spring, contemplating the long, empty dog-days of summer ahead and possibly hoping for a two-week respite from parenting, my father raised the possibility of sending me to summer camp.

I was, admittedly, a shy, reclusive and somewhat peculiar only child. He probably felt it would do me some good—bring me out of myself—and I am sure his intentions were entirely for the best.

My mother, a fervently Catholic woman, opposed the plan on the grounds that I might fetch up in some rustic, heathen Babylon where suitable Sunday observances were not available, thereby endangering my immortal soul. Also, she correctly assumed that I would put up a fight.

I, cowering in my room while the debate raged below, prayed that Mother's arguments would prevail—prayed that some patron saint of frankly peculiar children would deliver me from the misery of two weeks away from home.

Dear, safe home.

What was I so afraid of? Let me itemize.

Food was the first big issue. What would I find on my plate? Would there be casseroles containing concealed liver and other entrails? (So good for children!) Would I be forced to sit at the table until I had cleaned my plate? Would I gag? Might I vomit? Would everybody laugh?

Then there was the spectre of arts-and-crafts sessions. I feared that leather work, knot-tying and other arcane mysteries would feature largely in the compulsory curriculum. Having already failed at tying my Brownie tie, this was a daunting prospect. Having vomited the loathsome bread pudding, I would next have to produce some cunningly braided leather item and fail to do so to camp standards. I envisioned strapping, tanned counsellors rolling their eyes and whispering in covens behind my back about my inability to master the sheep-shank with double twist-turn manoeuvre. I was all thumbs.

Insomnia was another source of anxiety in my young life. Suppose that in the endless, loon-haunted darkness I lay awake, hour upon hour, night after night, until I finally collapsed, my health broken and my mind permanently addled by lack of sleep. In the cold light of dawn I would finally have to be taken away to an asylum for ruined children.

Privies, of course, bothered me. I hated and feared all bad smells and varmints. What if a spider dropped on my head? What if I slipped into the hole? And, once again, would I gag and vomit? "Beeeu—there's the girl who barfed in the john," they would say.

Which brings me to the fourth great phobia.

*Them*—the junior capos who run the social underground in these rustic gulags. *They* are the bully-princesses who have always abounded in Grade 6 female society. Their hair is perfect, their clothes ditto and *They* decide who is in and who is condemned to the outer darkness, the subject of ridicule, whispers and ostracism. I knew instinctively on which side of the great divide I would fall. *They* are still with us, under a veneer of social civility, a thin one. You know who you were—and are. Repent.

Phobia No. 5 was my fear of sports. I knew that aquatics were bound to be a big part of the program. I swam like a cat and deeply dreaded being forced into a canoe and taught the doubtless useful art of surviving a dumping in mid-lake.

Only slightly less horrible was softball. I had had some experience with the game, swatting ineffectually at the ball or standing, sun-blinded, in the heat-shimmering outfield. Voices shrilling at me "Get it, catch it, throw it!! Not that way, silly!" Being chosen last and reluctantly.

And, over all, I was phobic about the heart-sickening prospect of two weeks devoid of privacy, solitude, blessed reading time. I had a gut instinct that books were not highly regarded as a suitable pastime and that bookish kids came just after rabies-riddled raccoons in the pecking order. Oh yes . . . I was an odd child, indeed.

In the end, Mother and St. Eustace, patron saint of decidedly odd children, prevailed. I did not go to camp.

"Pity," you might say, "it may have helped her." What does not kill makes you stronger . . .

But guess what? With time and tender mercy, I got better all on my own. I now live a life replete with friends and abounding with joys. I am no longer shy. I even do some sports, though leatherwork still escapes me. *Tant pis.*

My final word?

Summer camp.

Shy kids.

Don't force 'em on each other.

*Alexandra Shea*
Kanata, Ont.

## TO SERVE AND PERPLEX

At first, I thought she was making fun of us.

When two friends and I appeared without reservations at the Tea Lobby of Victoria's Empress Hotel, the young woman hovering at the door smiled a wide-open smile.

This could be trouble, I thought.

Overstated and a bit crazed, it was the exact smile I usually get from people who think I've overstepped my expectations of good service, and who then proceed to show me strained (but markedly visible) sympathy as they explain how they'd *like* to help me—really, they would—but that their corporate policy dictates other-wise, or their shift is almost over, or the computer won't allow it, or I'm just plain not going to get what I'm willing to pay for.

"No reservations?" she said. "Well, that shouldn't be a problem!" (I include the exclamation mark, because she did, too.) She then began to scan the bustling room in which we stood, whose every overstuffed easy chair appeared already taken—and whose last sitting for tea was about to end in 15 minutes.

"There's a table almost free over there," she offered, before adding conspiratorially, "I know what it's like when you want to take tea and there's no room at the inn."

Was she being sarcastic, I wondered, and cast my friends a sideways glance.

Apparently not. Starting with her insistence that we follow her to our table—"but take your time to notice the view"—the service at the Empress went from considerate to accommodating to what bordered on indulgent.

And as it did so, my vague discomfort with it, I noticed, grew in direct proportion.

As we settled into our chairs, one of my friends commented on the ornateness of the china. "It was origi-nally presented to George V," offered our server, a middle-aged woman who seemed to appear out of nowhere, "and first used here for the visit of George VI and Queen Elizabeth, now the Queen Mother. . . . I hope you have a wonderful tea with us today, and you should have waited for me to pull out your chairs."

"Weird," said my other friend, as our server slipped away to get us our tea. "I know," I answered under my breath. "I feel a bit . . . confused."

And then back she came, sporting a tiered tray of sandwiches and scones, cream and jam. She asked us where we were from, chatted about how proud she was of the Empress's clotted cream—"from Jersey, not Devon, a real treat"—and then left us to eat.

"I'll trade you my cucumber sandwiches for your salmon ones," I whispered to my tablemates, the second she turned her back—at which point she whirled around full circle, a look of what might be called amused horror on her face. "There's no need to trade anything," she intoned. "More cucumber sandwiches coming up."

And come up they did, along with more salmon ones, in fact. No 89-cent surcharge for McSuper Size, no menu insert outlawing substitutes, no clucking of the tongue at a special request—no need to make a request at all.

And best of all, no attitude.

Seeing my camera on the table, she then offered to take our picture, and when she took off her glasses, I could see how tired she was, even though her eyes were smiling. "This will give you a nice memory of the day," she said. "You all look great."

"Okay," I said to my friends as she disappeared again, "now I'm feeling kind of stoned. Why is everyone here so nice?"

And that's when it hit me—the reason for my semi-flustered bafflement. It was simple, really: I was paying money for a service in our much-vaunted service economy—and I was getting it. Here, in the rarefied atmosphere of the Empress Tea Room, surrounded by brocade curtains and antique chandeliers and dour portraits of long-dead royals, I was . . . being served. And I was so unused to good service that I had felt suspicion, then confusion, and now, simply, a bit of heady nirvana.

Years of surly servers, clued-out temps, buck-passing answering machines and snickering functionaries flashed before my eyes—Sympatico phone reps unable or unwilling to solve the simplest of Internet glitches; gruff men in subway ticket booths finishing their personal phone calls before deigning to even look my way; waiters who ask if I'd like water, and then never remember to bring it; the gas-line guy who spray-painted—*spray-painted!*—my brick walk last week, then gave me an 800 number to call if it was such a big deal.

I know this may all make me sound like an A-1 crank—a waiter's worst nightmare, the nemesis of receptionists everywhere. In fact, the opposite is true: I've become so inured to bad service that I've learned to smile when I get it, put my tail between my legs, tip appropriately and be on my way.

And yes, I know Victoria is a tourist town. I know it's painted and clipped and pruned to appeal to those who go there to spend their hard-earned money. And I know tea at the Empress is, pure and simple, a not-inexpensive capitalist exchange. But how nice, for once, to pay my money and get what I paid for—how old-fashioned, it suddenly seemed, to make a straightforward market exchange, and not be sniffed at, shortchanged or just plain ignored.

By the time we were done tea, the rest of the room was empty. No one hovered, no one cleared their throats. In fact, the maître d' came by to make sure we took our time. "This is tea," he said, "no rushing allowed."

Leaving the hotel minutes later, the world slammed back into our faces, quite literally, when the tourist in front of us pulled the door open for himself, and then let it crash back on us. Walking around Victoria later that afternoon, we came across a brick wall in an alley, on which was spray-painted what must have been the work of a very disgruntled waiter. "Tipping," it read in a demented scrawl, "is 15 to 20 per cent."

How apt, I thought. Just expect it, just demand it, just stomp your foot and say it must be so. But heaven forbid you earn it. I mean, why bother? After all, if most customers are like me, they'll probably think something's terribly wrong should the service, for once, be right.

*Victor Dwyer*
Toronto, Ont.

## HOW LOW WILL YOU GO?

I recently caught a friend off guard by asking him, "What's your minimum go-down?"

"Huh?" he said.

"What's the smallest amount of money you'll reach down to pick up off the pavement?" I continued.

That got him thinking. He admitted to having stooped for nickels, a little below my range.

I'm a 25-cent-or-more guy, a quarter being the least I'll dip for. That's cost me plenty the past while, as I must have passed over a jillion dimes. Those little silver suckers are everywhere. Seems every time I step out the door—which I've been doing a lot lately—there's a dime sitting on the sidewalk in search of a warm pocket.

A dime isn't going to change my life substantially, but it might make some kid's day, so let him have it. When I was little, finding a dime was something for the family to discuss over dinner. Dad might even have demanded a share for "the college fund."

There's another reason for discounting dimes. No coin is as hard to pick up as a dime, the thinnest and smallest one we use. I've often wondered why it gets short shrift. Typically, the bigger the coin, the greater the value. So why is a dime only half the size of a nickel, but worth twice as much? Doesn't figure.

Furthermore, over the winter months, when the pavement is covered in snow and ice, picking up dimes is a near impossibility. Don't know about you, but I'm not prepared to wait until spring to pounce.

Despite the inclement weather, I've been getting out a lot the past while, walking an average of two hours a day, trying to get in shape. It's paid big dividends, as I've dropped about a dozen pounds, which makes stooping that much simpler.

I used to read or dabble with the daily crossword while afoot, a skill I cultivated over the years (though an occasional run-in with a telephone pole or parking meter was inevitable).

No more.

One of the more enlightened religions says that you shouldn't try multi-tasking in your daily life. When eating dinner, don't watch television or pet the cat. Just eat. Likewise, when out for a stroll, just walk.

But I still have this habit of moving with my head down, even without a magazine or crossword to tempt me. All the walking books say that is a no-no, that the best way to improve your posture while out and about is to keep your head upright.

Yet, there are benefits to having your head bowed, as suggested already. You aren't likely to discover a new planet even if your noggin is aimed at the heavens. But you'll find lots of loose change—and bills, too—by emulating a certain Notre Dame bellringer.

My biggest prize this winter has been a $10 bill. My mother lode came on Christmas day (a chiller, you may recall) while en route to a friend's house for breakfast. The bill was sitting atop a snowbank, probably having fallen from someone's purse or pocket. No one was around, so I claimed it.

It wasn't mine for long.

As I was approaching the corner of Toronto's College and Yonge, a fellow who was in a bad way—he looked like he'd been out all night—asked if I could spare a dollar for a coffee. Instead, I took him inside the nearby donut shop, bought us both a cup with my newfound "dixie," then handed him the change.

It made his day. Mine, too.

You should know that bills aren't that commonplace. But coins seem to tumble from the sky for me: not just those dreaded dimes and more manageable quarters, but loonies and toonies. Subway tickets and tokens often materialize, too.

A note on the tickets: they are invariably in a bad way, spattered and tattered, but until now they have got me aboard without someone asking, "Hey buddy, did you scrape your windshield with this?"

My biggest find happened a few years ago, before I started walking in earnest. About a block from home, I noticed what looked like a $50 bill poking out of the snow. It was as advertised.

However, I was heavily into the Ontario sports lottery at that time, so I rushed off to invest my 50. I didn't come up with a single winner. Maybe that'll inspire the people who pen the plugs for our provincial lotteries: "From 50 to zero in an afternoon."

You may have noticed a pattern to my many finds. They invariably come in the winter months, often on the heels of a heavy snowfall. Many folks are butter-fingered by nature. Drop the thermometer a few degrees and they literally lose touch, especially when fumbling for coins and the like.

To compound their problems, there's almost no hope of reclaiming a coin from a snowbank. It's like a golfer trying to track down his ball in fall, when the fairways are covered in leaves. (As an aside, I should tell you that I'm also good at finding golf balls.)

So, stop your day-trading and get outside.

That's where the real money is to be found.

By the way, but what is your minimum go-down?

*Larry Humber*
Toronto, Ont.

# LAWN ORDER: THE SOD MANIFESTOS

Springtime and a young man's fancy turns to, well, lawn maintenance.

I never cared for grass myself, maybe because I have an allergic reaction to it. But all around my old neighbourhood in Beaverton, Ont., there was an unspoken dialogue between neighbours that took the form of large green semaphores. Careful cutting of your lawn told the world: "Hey, I'm a good citizen. I care about property values."

Everyone around me had big gas mowers or tractors. I preferred my humble electric mower. It wasn't fancy but it was environmentally sound. My neighbours cut their lawns once a week. I did mine once a month, whether it needed it or not. Unlike them I sprayed it neither with poisons nor water. It grew how and when it wanted. The kids played on it and the guinea pigs ate it.

People would stroll by and shake their heads when they saw my lawn. I had crabgrass, the cancer of lawn care. At first I felt guilty. But Nature herself delivered the final judgment. Because my yard was like an oasis in a sterile sea of green, I found we had frogs and toads and the occasional garter snake to keep them hopping. I let corners of the yard go wild and little purple flowers took over. A cardinal built a home in our wild cedar hedge. I felt I had balanced the natural order with the neighbourhood grass code.

Then a couple I'll call Robert and Karen moved in next door. They were a nice young pair with every toy imaginable: plane, boat, Ski-Doo and tractor. Robert, with a religious zeal, liked to cut his lawn every other day. As for me, my lawn sins were not confined to any one season. I had read somewhere that leaves should be left on the ground as long as possible to allow the nutrients to leach back into the soil and to give cover for bugs that migrating birds feed upon. Robert believed that you must keep the green beacon of good neighbourliness shining at all times, and so he went at the leaves on a daily basis. Soon the front of his house was fortified with clear plastic bags full of leaves. After the last leaf fell I composted mine in the back corner of my yard beneath a huge pine tree.

Fate couldn't have planned a more mismatched set of neighbours. He was getting rich quickly the 21st-century way with computers. I was going poor slowly the 19th-century way as a teacher and author. We lived in different worlds. They grew a cedar hedge to block out their view of mine. We presented sod manifestos.

I believed in tolerance and diversity. Weeds and wild-flowers cohabited. My lawn had to be viewed up close, a few centimetres at a time. I was always discovering some tiny marvel in the grass.

Robert looked down upon his yard from a great distance. He believed in uniformity and discipline. His property was a triumph of man over nature. Robert imposed his will upon the land with heavy equipment and chemical warfare.

When the time came to sell our house, I had to cut the grass every week so it would show better. I was saddened to see that the frogs and toads went away. In the end the final offer came from . . . Robert and Karen. They had the money to buy us out. They said they would renovate our little cottage home and rent it. As part of the deal we would live in the place until our new house in Orillia was finished, but Robert was to be allowed access to the yard in the meantime.

After a summer of unnatural yard work, I was only too happy to let him have his way. My relief was short-lived. As I watched him run his tractor around the yard, shredding every bit of wildness out, it dawned on me. Robert hadn't wanted my house or the tiny beach that went with it. All he really wanted was my lawn.

The leaves soon fell and nearly every day he came over to bag them. Soon one side of my driveway was fortified with clear plastic bags full of leaves just like his. Robert didn't think much of my composting system and eradicated it. No doubt the migrating birds were confused. By November the lawn was leafless and lifeless. I had sold out Mother Nature.

Moving day came on Nov. 3. As we moved into the new house, the construction foreman came over to tell me that it was too late in the year to put down sod. I had to pretend to be really disappointed to show respect for universal lawn order. My new neighbour came over to introduce himself. To my horror, I discovered that he was a landscaper who also installed lawn sprinkler systems. Now I think I will put in interlocking stones everywhere rather than fight another neighbour turf war. I must accept that I fought the lawn and the lawn won.

*Michael Howell*
Orillia, Ont.

## LIFE LESSONS LEARNED ON VACATION

Last August, I borrowed my mother's second-hand Oldsmobile and drove for nine hours from Montreal to Cape May, New Jersey. In the car with me was Sam, who was six, and Jake, who was two at the time and had taken to referring to himself in the third person by his baptismal name, Jacob, which he pronounced Jay-cup. Anyway, back in August, I packed up my sons and our stuff in the borrowed car because we were going on vacation.

If the truth be known, I was taking the vacation as much for Sam and Jake to see the Atlantic Ocean as for me; I needed to prove something to myself and to the world, something about how I could do this single-parenting thing, how not only could I take care of the boys on my own, but how I could even take them on vacation to a seaside resort filled with my own happy childhood memories.

Our first stop on our way out of town was my parents' house.

"Here's a map," my father said. I accepted the map graciously, even though he knew, and I knew, that I could probably find my way just fine without it.

"And-here-don't-say-anything-just-take-it-call-me-when-you-get-there," my mother said, pressing five American twenties into the palm of my hand.

Fifty minutes later, as we crossed the American border into upstate New York, the rain began. No, make that, the torrential downpour, the deluge. Monsoon season. I gripped the steering wheel, clenched my teeth and drove. I can do this, I told myself. In the backseat, the boys huddled together under baby blankets and sang, ". . . *And the rain rain rain came down down down in rushing rising rivulets* . . ." along with a Winnie-the-Pooh tape. They thought they were hilarious.

Our second stop was in Glens Falls, N.Y., four hours later. Despite the driving rain and the windshield wipers going at geek-speed, I managed to spot a McDonald's just off Highway 87. The tires squealed along the slick pavement as I braked for the off ramp. My nerves were shot.

We spent an hour in the McDonald's in Glens Falls because even though it didn't have a ball room, it did have a self-serve soda fountain with an ice machine that sent square cubes ka-thunking into the boys' cups over and over again, and dispensable paper-covered straws. The boys ate cheeseburger happy meals and caramel sundaes while I picked at what they left behind on their trays in between sips of black coffee. On our way out, I steered them toward the restrooms.

"Mom," Sam said, lingering in front of the men's room, "we're boys, you know." I glanced, horrified, in Sam's direction.

"Look, Sam," I said, squatting down to look him in the eye, "I know you're boys, but I'm a girl. I can't go in there."

"Well, I can," he said, giving the door a shove.

"We're in a foreign country!" I shouted, as if this detail made some kind of difference. I squeezed Jake's hand and followed Sam through the door. Standing in front of the urinals, a man in a Yankees ball cap glanced over his shoulder at me and winked.

"Excuse us," I said.

Sam walked up to the wall of urinals. "What's that?" he said, pointing toward the drain.

"It's a urinal cake," the man said.

"Blecch," Sam said.

In Paramus, N.J., just before the entrance to the Garden State Parkway, I finally found our motel. I'd booked ahead—a Howard Johnson's right on the highway—so the boys and I could have a meal, some sleep, before starting out early the next morning for the final three-hour leg of our drive.

"Can we go swimming?" Sam asked as soon as we'd checked in. Jake, happy to be free of his car seat, bounced on the double bed.

"Tomorrow," I said.

Even though it was late in the day, the air was still warm and humid. After stashing our overnight bags, we set off on foot to find supper. But in new Fisher-Price sneakers, Jake tripped in front of a closed bagel shop and skinned both knees. Sam whacked a hand against the glass door. "I want a bagel," he said. "Let's break in."

"Sam," I said, scooping up a hysterical Jake in my arms, "we can't break in. We'll find somewhere to eat."

Sam swept his hand out in front of him. "Where? All I can see are used car lots and liquor barns and craft stores and closed bagel shops."

"We'll find something," I said, at that point not entirely sure we would.

Heading back in the other direction, I spied a large sign with an owl on it. Sam saw it too. "Hey, look Mom," he said. "An owl!" He struck off ahead of me and Jake, easily jumping the hedge that separated the used car lot from the Howard Johnson's parking lot. "Come on," he said. By the time Jake and I caught up with him, he was already holding open the door for us. He called it a friendly owl restaurant.

Inside, I eyed a woman straddling a barstool near the front door. "Welcome to Hooters," she said. She wagged two fingers at Jake. "He's so cute," she said.

To be honest, I didn't make the connection between the woman and the barstool and the owl immediately. I'd never even heard of Hooters before, and if I had I wouldn't have made it through the door, but because I hadn't, and because we were hungry, and because I was still trying to prove something to the world and to myself, I asked the hostess if they had a children's menu.

"We shore do," she replied.

"What's on it?" I asked suspiciously.

"PB & J sandwiches, chicken fingers, cheeseburgers."

"Cheeseburgers," Jake said.

The hostess took us to a table at the far end of the restaurant. A roll of paper towels on a dowel was in the centre of the table. Over the music, Sam shouted, "Look at all the TVs, Mom."

As Sam began counting the TVs (there must have been more than 50 of them, all tuned to different stations), Jake licked the ketchup bottle. He was hungry. Next to us, a table of men with long grey beards and leather jackets shared a huge plate of chicken wings as the waitress collected their empty beer pitchers.

On the wall facing me there was a sign that read: Caution, Blondes Thinking.

When Sam finished counting TVs, he leaned over and asked me why all the waitresses were wearing bathing suits.

I nodded. "There's a pool party later on," I said. "After work, they're all going swimming."

The waitress plunked down a big basket of curly fries and three grilled cheese sandwiches. Sam said, "We're going swimming tomorrow."

"Is that right?" the waitress asked.

Sam nodded. Then he smiled at me. "We're on vacation," he said, diving into the fries.

*Debbie Howlett*
St. Lambert, Que.

## WATER, WATER EVERYWHERE

It started a little more than a month ago. My partner Pete would grab his ball of string, with the nut attached to the end for an anchor, and head outside.

A few minutes later, he would return with his pronouncement: "It's up to my shoulders so we'll be okay for a while."

A week after that, he would report the progress, or lack thereof, claiming that it had dropped to his knees. "Time to call," he would say, "unless we get some rain in the next day or two."

Now I've never been one to wish for rain or even worry about it unless it was threatening to interfere with my plans. As a kid, I dreaded hearing my mom say she could feel the rain coming, in her bones. This prediction always seemed to be announced at a time when we had planned a day at the beach.

I'm not blessed with my mother's divining abilities but I do know how to use the phone. And so I placed the call. "Would that be for a pool?" the person on the other end asked.

Not likely, I thought, as I told her it was for drinking and just about everything else. Our conversation ended with an assurance the water truck would arrive before the end of the day.

While waiting for the truck, I couldn't help but think about how much I've taken water for granted. Most of my life I have lived on city services. The limits to use centred around our hot water tank's capacity. I've also lived around an abundance of water sources. Here in Canada's ocean playground, you're never far away from the sea and thousands of lakes dot this maritime landscape.

That all changed several years ago. We bought a house on the outskirts of Halifax and never once thought to ask if there was enough water in the well. We found out the hard way after a long weekend visit from a friend and his family. We had flushed our way out of this basic necessity of life.

I panicked that first time, not realizing you could order truckloads of water. "We'll have to drill," I had said as did everyone else around me. But then we did the math. My house is across from the ocean and many homeowners have been known to hit salt a few times before striking the real

stuff. This costs thousands of dollars without any guaran-
tees. There's also talk about uranium in these parts, which
would mean additional costs to install a pump to filter the
bad stuff.

We decided instead to learn to live with our limited
water supply and pay for the occasional truckload. Two rain
barrels under the eavestroughs collect water for the garden.
When that water runs out, the plants go without. We know
of what we speak when we tell house guests to leave it
mellow if it's yellow. Forget laundry. That gets done in
town. No running the tap when you brush and be quick
in the shower. Baths just have to wait until winter.

Within hours of placing the order, the big shiny truck
came barrelling up the hill with water literally spilling
out of its metal seams. I lifted off the well cover feeling a
bit embarrassed. My neighbours now know I am without
water again this year while they are safe in the comfort of
their drilled wells. Part of me envies how they can run their
sprinklers at night or wash their cars without thinking
about it.

The embarrassment passed quickly for I got caught up
in the moment. I watched as the driver connected a hose to
the truck and dragged the other end to the base of the well.
And then, shortly thereafter, water began to fill the empty
hole. I had noticed a crack in the hose where water was
leaking into the driveway. So I asked the driver if I could
move that part of the hose over my garden to take advan-
tage of all that water just running away. He obliged. Within

10 minutes, it all wrapped up. He filled up my rain barrel for good measure and I handed over the $100 cheque. I knew it was a small price to pay.

Now for the next phase. You see, filling up the well that way disturbs all the sediment. It will take a few days before the water settles. Until then, the water comes out brown. We can't drink it; neither is a shower that refreshing, since I can't help but feel like I'm washing in a mud puddle. But this, too, shall pass. Sure enough, I hear Pete say: "It's just about clear. One more day ought to do it."

Finally that day arrives. The water is clear and rain is in the air, or so my mother says. If we're lucky, we'll only have to go through this one more time before the snow comes. I do take some comfort in going through this, year after year. For one thing, I've learned first-hand the value of water, which puts me ahead of those who have yet to realize the limits of this resource. With boil-water orders, e-coli scares and other water concerns making the news daily and talk about selling Canada's water supply, it's just a matter of time before most of us will face such realities.

Now, wouldn't you know, as I finish writing about my water woes, the sound of rain is all around me. I hear Pete in the background saying we'll be fine for a while with radio reports forecasting rain throughout the week.

So much for those beach plans.

*Angela Power Poirier*
Shad Bay, N.S.

## GROWING VEGETABLES
## AND SHOOTING HOOPS

I spend a lot of time in my neighbourhood park in down-town Toronto, mostly working in the gardens or baking at the outdoor wood-fired oven there.

Over the years, I've met many young people who also spend a lot of time at the park, playing basketball or just "chilling" with their friends. Sometimes those young folks have done odd jobs for the park, baking at the oven or cleaning up the park or helping out with community campfires.

People often ask me: Have the things we do in our park "rehabilitated" any young people who formerly made trouble? The short answer is yes. Certainly we now have very little damage (such as graffiti or vandalism) in the park, and there seems to be a code about fights in the park: "We don't fight here and we don't let other people come and fight here. We help keep this park safe." That's their theory and, while not strictly adhered to by everyone, it more or less carries the day.

The longer answer is complicated. The young people who come and hang around, particularly in the proximity of the basketball court, have a strong sense of themselves as a separate culture, insiders with everyone else on the outside. In that way, their sense of themselves is parallel with many other people who use the park: the middle-class older folks who have a strong sense that we are the insiders, the legitimate people who behave well.

The sharp separations mean that if the older folks in the park come and try to act friendly with the young guys, they are often rebuffed, sometimes very rudely. The young guys tell them to get lost, and the older folks are appalled at their manners. There continues to be a lot of pretty graphic swearing, and if we hadn't disconnected the electrical power outlet near the basketball courts, we would still be hearing a lot of uncensored music that blasts out rape-and-violence songs across the park. There is a fondness for the "ghetto" look—lots of litter and periodic binges of breaking glass. This kind of stuff is cyclical, but seemingly not much under the control of parks staff or other park users.

The various social circles that form around the bake ovens or the campfire circle (this includes the outdoor music and theatre rehearsals that are often in our park) are so near the basketball court that the different scenes can't help but overlap. The cooking fires/ovens were added after the young guys had established themselves. The overlap grates continually, because of the forced proximity of unmatched groups. Neither side chooses to be near the other, but the young guys very much want the basketball court and the older people (and their little kids) very much want the cooking fires. Or the older people very much want the fresh air of their evening walk through the park (some of the most beautiful flowerbeds are also near this part of the park) and the young guys very much want their evening campfire, where they can drink and maybe roast hot dogs. So they are constantly forced into each other's grating presence.

This "grating" is actually rather productive, even if sometimes painfully so. I learned the usefulness of such proximity from a wonderful essay written by the Norwegian criminologist Nils Christie, called Conflict as Property, and it treats conflict as a precious, practical community resource for summoning up the gifts of the people who live there. Christie wrote about the theft of this resource by lawyers, courts and others who take conflict out of a community and thereby prevent ordinary people from behaving with courage and generosity and ingenuity—important practical forms of spiritual exercise.

So: not long ago I was working in the vegetable garden beside the ovens and some of the young people were having a loud, scary discussion relating to sex and prison life, and involving a lot of graphic cursing. Neither of us could move to a different location, so there we were: me with my spade and they with their stories, a very light rain falling on us both.

I was forced to listen to things I would never have to listen to inside my house, inside my own social class, and they were forced to get intermittent glares from me. Eventually (after quite a while), the talk modified, toned down a bit, then stopped.

I saw some of them again the day after. I was revolted with them, and they were hostile to me, the middle-aged lady getting mixed up in their business. But I had a pizza-making group to attend to at the outdoor oven, and they had to play basketball, so we were forced to stay near each other.

Some of the older children in the pizza-making group went to watch the basketball, then they got their turn at one of the hoops and began to play too. One of the basketball players came over and played with them, because, he told me, kids like to play with a bigger guy, it makes them feel big. The parents at the oven were all busy talking to each other, and there was nothing about the scene to worry them. The usual swearing almost stopped, because of the code of not swearing near young children, but the basketball went on and the drinking went on and the pizzamaking went on. Everybody was having a good time.

At some point, well into the evening, one of the young guys walked by and made some friendly remark, and I noticed I wasn't angry anymore. There was such a pleasing, even joyful, normalcy about the scene that I couldn't feel that the end of civilized society had arrived, as I had the day before.

So: who was rehabilitated? Are the shocked older people like me also in need of rehabilitation? Or in need of forgiveness, for all the unfair advantages we routinely gain for ourselves and our group, and which we may try to explain away by pointing to the bad behaviour of others outside our group?

What I think I know is this: there have to be standards and that, in cities like Toronto, people have to learn to work out the standards across different groups. This work, ideally, is continually in progress and needs proximity. The campfires and bake oven in our park are an interesting, continuous prompt for such proximity.

For me, sometimes, such proximity makes me delight in the lively, quirky existence of people quite unlike me.

On good days, they do me the honour of delighting in me as well.

*Jutta Mason*
Toronto, Ont.

## NEW FIELDS OF DISTANT FORTUNE

Five years ago, my dad wished me good adventures and left me standing outside a tiny apartment building with white stucco walls, just across the street from the University of Saskatchewan.

The sky was darkening by the time dad pulled away and he still had a long drive ahead of him. The day had been long for both of us—we had left home just as the orange morning sun glinted off the neat row of metal granaries in our yard, but the glare didn't stop me from looking back.

Everything was just as it should be. The large picture window in the living room was neatly hidden behind bushes of some sort (I watched them grow but still didn't know what type they were). Three white pillars stood proudly as they held up the neatly shingled roof. The rows of flowers planted in front of the house by my own hands were just past their peak. In the kitchen's bay window, I could make out a figure, just the size of my mom, watching the truck pull out of the yard.

I turned back around, no longer able to see because of the tears that were filling my eyes, and the diesel engine that kept putting distance between my home and my future. Quickly wiping the tears away and not saying anything, I resumed my fixated stares, this time out the side window and into the endless nothingness of fields and fields and fields.

Dad, likewise, said nothing. He, too, was busy looking into the space that surrounded us, but his purpose was to spot that one wild oat standing defiantly above the heads of his golden wheat and not to cram in the last perfect view of eternity.

I turned my gaze to the truck. With one paranoid peek over my shoulder, I reassured myself that every box was still roped in. Inside, the truck was not so neat—dusty, always dusty. The floormats were covered with so many clumps of dirt and piles of grain that it would take only a few good waterings to harvest a bumper crop in the cab.

I sneezed, just like I always do in this dust. Dad looked over with a smirk and guffaw. I've been witness to that enough to know what it means: "Not a farm girl." I smirked back, holding in another sneeze and hoping the smell of dad's coffee would choke out any more dust particles.

Dad's large calloused fingers awkwardly fiddled with the radio. AM, of course. And just as he settled in on his favourite drone of voices on CBC 540, I began nesting for a snooze to help pass the next four hours.

But just as I shut my eyelids, dad opened his mouth.

He talked about 1963. As a younger Gerald, he was a student in the College of Agriculture at the University of Saskatchewan. He lived in the upper apartment of an old Victorian-style house. He ate a lot of peanut-butter sandwiches and could cook hot dogs and macaroni-and-cheese all in the same pot.

He made the frigid trek each morning over the North Saskatchewan River on the University Bridge and returned that same way every night. He took physics and chemistry and economics and studied in the library. He liked to wear turtlenecks and he smoked a pipe.

As dad talked, the fields outside became smaller and the hills not so far apart. More and more trees took the place of wheat. Then farmhouses were replaced with strip malls and pastures with parking lots.

And the four-hour trip had passed as quickly as the 18 years leading up to that drive.

Dad pulled the truck into the back alley of College Drive and expertly backed up onto the driveway. Then he with one box and I with another moved silently from truck to building and repeated the routine until there was nothing left to carry.

And just as dad climbed into the truck and was about to shut the door, I opened my mouth.

I talked about 1996. I would be a student in the College of English at the University of Saskatchewan. I would eat a lot of peanut butter and learn the wonder of Hamburger Helper. I would walk through the cold Saskatchewan winters to my classes each morning and then back again each night. I would study in the same room as my dad once did and I would find myself.

But I came dangerously close to forgetting that vision. I thought, five years and 3,000 kilometres later, that taking my education to Toronto and beginning a career there was a Significant Demonstration of Independence. I held no resentment toward my Prairie upbringing and small-town morals, but I did believe they were holding me back. So I fought back tears and stubbornly headed in the direction of opportunity.

But then, during a frantic phone call home about finances and car insurance, dad reminded me of something.

"I'm proud of you," he said.

With my mouth gaping open and my eyes slowly filling with tears, I listened as my dad told me I showed a lot more gumption than he ever had at my age. He said I had done well, going so far away, getting a job and tackling responsibilities. And as I listened to this man who has been ploughing Prairie ground since he was my age, bravely facing stormy weather, drought and infestations, I realized I never have to prove myself to him, because everything that I am is everything that he is—and that is nothing to run away from.

I smiled, maybe not as a farm girl, but as my father's daughter.

*Gillian Girodat*
Shaunavon, Sask.

## RETURN TO A SHATTERED CITY

It's taken me a while to return to my Manhattan neighbourhood. The place where I lived was in the financial district. Built in 1911, the building was used to store documents and to house small factories until, in the 1990s, it was converted into loft apartments. For three hours there, on Sept. 11, I was trapped in my apartment while the sky rained melting metal, debris from the airplanes, clothing without people in them, and the pulverized concrete of those stunning buildings, the two towers.

Just 48 hours after the attack, my fiancé and I were on the train to Toronto with our worldly belongings, consisting of the clothes on our backs and our passports. When we crossed the border at Niagara Falls, the Canadian

Immigration officer offered us his place if we had nowhere else to go. I was home indeed.

But we had to go back to New York.

So two weeks later we are on the plane. I read the emergency procedure manual like I'm cramming for a final exam. We study the blonde flight attendant and measure the likelihood of her taking down a potential hijacker. We don't like the odds. As our plane descends, we peer out the window, wondering if the city has returned to its usual brashness.

It is different. Our taxi driver at LaGuardia Airport does the hitherto unimaginable: he leaps out of his seat, grabs our bags, holds the back door open and warmly says, "Welcome to New York." As we drive into the city, we see a skyline dominated by the Empire State Building. We see American flags draped on every major building; people hold them in their hands as they walk down the street, as if for protection.

The first night, we stay in mid-town. The next day, we make our way down to our old neighbourhood. The streets that once led to the World Trade Center are now thronged with tourists, army vehicles and police officers at each corner. I can't bring myself to look up; it's empty space.

At the checkpoint on Broadway and Fulton Streets, we surrender our passports, other identification and proof of residence. The police officer explains that he will escort us to our building and remain for the 15 minutes we are allowed to gather our things. He's grouchy after working

20-hour days for the past 13 days. When we ask how he is doing, he shrugs.

Just a half block on, the streets are littered with dump trucks, cranes, tractors, medical service stations. Each police and fire station has its own tent. The men are slumped in chairs. Their outer gear is slicked over in mud and debris, their eyes expressionless as we tramp past in stunned silence.

At the corner of Church and Liberty Streets, we pause for a minute and stare up at the Deutsche Bank building which stands in the single block that separates our home and the WTC. A 30-storey section of a WTC tower facade is wedged at a 60-degree angle into its front side. I shudder to think what that chunk of metal could have done to my apartment building while I was inside.

Down the next block, we walk by the high school, now spray-painted with the word "morgue." Around one more corner, we see our building, surrounded with generators and tanker trucks with cleaning solvents to wash away asbestos residue. Inside, we hug the doorman and superintendent before racing up a flight of stairs. The stench from the refrigerator brings tears to our eyes. The floor is littered with soot.

Now I remember the hours I spent here that morning. Minutes after the first implosion, when I dared to open the door to my hallway, I saw two bleeding firemen. They had been standing at the base of Tower Two when they were picked up by the blast and launched into the lobby of my building. They had managed to crawl up a flight of stairs and were lying there in the hall, cocooned in inches of debris. Another tenant and I had used T-shirts and bed linens to make splints for their broken arms. We kept changing the layers of gauze as they bled through them.

Today, we have only 15 minutes in the apartment. We turn the desk upside down, looking for insurance documents and banking statements. We throw clothes into a duffel bag. I stuff photos into my pockets, grab jewellery and ram it into my socks. We toss rotting meat from the freezer into a garbage bag along with the leftovers from the dinner we had the night of Sept. 10.

We're despondent as we trudge back to the periphery to retrieve our passports and identification. I am no longer polite as we shove our way through the crowds of curious onlookers. I'm angry that they're taking pictures of where my neighbourhood once stood.

The World Trade Center once held my bank, drugstore, bookstore, coffee shop and newsstand. I caught the subway to and from work there, purchased flowers on the way home, bought Christmas presents from the Gap, and laughed at the businessmen staring longingly at the window displays of Victoria's Secret.

Now, I don't know if those businessmen are even alive. Nor do I know what happened to the two firemen whose wounds I helped patch up. I do not know what happened to the elderly woman from the ninth floor I found in my hallway, sobbing that her husband Barry had gone for the newspaper at the very minute of the first attack.

What I do know is that the entire squad on duty that day at Fire Station 10 at the end of my street is likely dead. And that a friend is mourning the loss of her father, uncle and two cousins. And ultimately, my world is changed by forces that I cannot begin to understand. God bless America, but I'll be coming home to Canada.

*Karen Mah*
Toronto, Ont.

## ACCORDION DREAMS
## IN THE PARK ON A SATURDAY

There's an inner accordionist lurking inside all of us. This was only one of many truths I learned during a recent community yard-sale in a downtown Toronto park. Used clothes don't sell at any price. Thanks to bank machines, $20 bills are the most common currency unit, even for purchases under a dollar. And lots of babies are being born: the crib, toddler bed and playpen sold instantly.

This annual event was also a great way to take the pulse of a neighbourhood in transition, in a setting that was more ancient outdoor bazaar than modern shopping mall. Early Saturday morning, we drove our packed car through the historic gates of the original Trinity College, Bishop

Strachan's centre of higher learning in 19th-century Anglican Toronto. Tennis courts, playgrounds and drinking fountains designed for thirsty dogs as well as dog-walkers have replaced those gothic halls, as well as almost 100 tables which lined the curving roads through the park on this particular day.

Prime spots under trees were already taken by the time we set up shop. But we were near enough to the community barbecue and the public washrooms to attract plenty of browsers and buyers. Friends we hadn't seen for months added to the festive atmosphere as we caught up on neighbourhood news. We debated the pros and cons of yet more loft conversions in the area and the opening of high-end interior design stores and an oyster bar around the corner. Karen and Stefan are moving to Helsinki for a year. Natalka is having an exhibit of her paintings this fall. Martha and Scott's baby has just started walking. Paula shared her sunscreen. Even people we didn't know joined in the conversations. But the real reason for being there was commerce. The bartering, bargaining banter, the exchange of goods and money that made the hours fly by and kept the customers coming. Even our nine-year-old daughter, initially a reluctant partner, was getting into the event. Trade in her old toys and books was brisk at 25 cents apiece and, the next thing I knew, she was making change for bigger purchases I'd had no hand in at all.

The decision to part with some of the clutter in one's daily life is always tempered with sentimentality and the knowledge that every object has a story.

Like the accordion.

It's not a great story of de Maupassant pathos or Leacock wit, simply a tale of impulse: the purchase of a Marco d'Oro accordion in a flea market in Pennsylvania more than 10 years ago. The accordion came to symbolize all the untested talents and uncharted avenues of my life. Learn to play the accordion and I'd discover my true identity as a singing, swinging squeeze-box mama. I imagined kitchen parties where all my friends would suddenly be playing fiddles, guitars and spoons and then we'd hit the road, busking our way around the world with music in our souls and our children step-dancing to the beat.

Alas, the road to finding my inner McGarrigle sister has not been travelled and I decided to bring the accordion along as an attention-grabber even if it didn't sell. I hadn't anticipated the magical spell an accordion casts over people. Chinese, Italian, Portuguese, French, Arabic, Ukrainian, a neighbour from Newfoundland—everyone wanted to embrace that pearlized case and tickle its vertical keyboard. I longed to hear *Lady of Spain* or *Lara's Theme* from *Doctor Zhivago* or anything with a Cajun rhythm. But for all the attention the accordion drew, no one knew how to play it!

The day was a huge success. We sold all of the stuff worth selling at bargain-basement prices. The larger or heavier the item, the lower we were willing to go. We gave away sun hats, fistfuls of pens and pencils, an old quilt and a grandmother's ancient stepstool to friends, new and old.

I took payment for a small bike in the form of a pre-scratched lottery ticket apparently worth $4.

Our old push lawn mower found a new home with a 12-year-old boy who offered a toonie but got it for free.

In the end, it was Dave who bought the accordion. Dave who kept coming back again and again. Dave who admitted he'd never played any instrument. Dave who promised he'd return to the park next year and play a tune. For 50 bucks, I happily parted with my dreams.

And, best of all, because I was anchored to our table all day, I didn't have time to shop.

*Jane French*
Toronto, Ont.

## NO REAL DREAD OF A SQUARE HEAD

If genes had the final word I'd be French Canadian. I was born and raised in Ottawa to French-Canadian parents where I attended French Catholic grade school followed by public French high school. Then something that would have a profound impact on my identity occurred: when I was 16, I got a job at a family camp popular with the local Anglo-Saxon crowd where, skin colour aside, I was a token minority.

Following that summer, allegiance to my French-Canadian friends from De La Salle gave way to English friends at Glebe Collegiate. It wasn't entirely a case of preferring English over French. I was simply exploring new possibilities: the pals I chose to spend less time with had been with me since pre-kindergarten, although I'd be lying if I didn't admit to enjoying a certain freedom with my new-found Anglo buddies. They weren't bound by the linguistic guilt that French kids grow up with in Ottawa, the constant harping of teachers in the halls to speak French, the imposition of seemingly "boring" French culture to counteract the omnipresence of English. I wasn't terribly interested in being French Canadian as far as language and culture were concerned. Nevertheless, while co-opting as much Englishness from my new milieu as I could, being *"homme grenouille"* was my trump card, my way to a unique identity within this adoptive gang.

Despite some members having fractional amounts of Latin blood in their veins, this group had never included a bona fide French Canadian. Although fluently bilingual, I was apt to betray my roots with some pretty creative sentence structures and pronunciations worthy of Jean Chrétien—a source of great amusement to the tribe many times. This, and my willingness to go along, was all it took to re-christen me "Frenchie." By the time I moved to Montreal to study at Concordia University, it had become my name. There are acquaintances I knew for years who didn't know my proper name is Paul. This began to grate, but I didn't do anything about it. That is, until my father found out.

It happened one snowy day during the Christmas school break about seven years ago. One of my friends tried to get my attention in public: "Frenchie!" he cried at the top of his lungs in a crowded ski shop. My father, who was with me on this excursion, was far from impressed. In fact, he was mortified. This nickname conjured unpleasant memories of teasing back when he was a teen in Cornwall, Ont., attending an English high school—in the fifties, when there was no constitutional guarantee to French high-school education. I was castigated and he categorically forbade me from accepting this designation. To him, it could be nothing but pejorative.

I found his argument compelling (if not the intensity of his disappointment). And so it would no longer be. I simply wouldn't answer when addressed in the offensive manner. At times, I had to be more explicit, often by recounting of the ski-shop anecdote. It took a while. Eventually, it stopped. At least in my presence. These guys still form the core of my friends and I know some of them still call me "Frenchie" behind my back. It is mostly used as a term of endearment but, to this day, I can't help but feel that there's an undercurrent of colonial condescension.

And now for the flip side: I lived in Montreal from its economic nadir of the early '90s through the referendum of '95 and ultimately fled the ugliness for what I thought would be the rational sanctum of Toronto. My move to the centre of the universe was purportedly to get a film career started but I ended up a bilingual customer-service representative at a mutual fund company. I had just spent seven years living a predominantly English life in Montreal only to end up working mostly in French in Toronto. Interesting. My spoken French had always been very good. Now it was bordering on excellent.

I got homesick for Montreal roughly at the same time my mutual fund career was simply making me sick (figuratively, of course). I decided to rekindle my ambition to work in film. Yes, there is plenty of film work in Toronto but Montreal was where I wanted to be: quite frankly, I was looking forward to working on French film sets. I find their atmosphere simply more enjoyable than those in the rest of Canada. At least to me.

I've since had the pleasure of working on an all-Quebec production where the lingua franca is French. But most of my work has been on American or English-Canadian productions. These are characterized by an incredible mixture of French and English where some key personnel and actors speak only English, some only French and most, some degree of both. This is not a problem for me, of course, since I can morph from one cultural platform to another. Well, almost.

When I left Toronto I felt confident that my French was beyond reproach. I was ready to return to the cradle of Frenchness and to be embraced as French Canadian. I've been back 18 months and, to my horror, I continue to get this from my fellow compatriots: "*Ein. Tu parles dont bien français pour un anglo.*" ("You sure speak French well for an Anglo.") This stings.

I was dismayed to learn that being Franco-Ontarian doesn't quite cut the mustard here. Language alone isn't enough. I underestimated the vastness of the rich cultural vocabulary one must learn to pass as a native Montrealer. I'm working on it, but suspect that I will always come up somewhat short.

Not having a strong, inclusive sense of cultural identity makes me feel uneasy at times. In any large assembly of Québécois it is readily apparent that I'm not "one of them." And on the other side of the divide I can feel equally marginalized. I have grown up lacking the cultural signifiers that land me squarely in one camp or the other. In Quebec, English Canadians are often referred to affectionately as "*têtes carrées*"—square heads. The biggest concession I've been given thus far is that I'm a "*tête carrée avec les coins arrondis.*" A square head with rounded corners.

I guess, until further notice, this will have to do.

*Paul Drouin*
Montreal, Que.

# A DOCTOR WRITES FROM ZIMBABWE

Dear Canada:

Are you still there? A funny question, you may think, as you settle down to your morning paper with a cup of coffee or maybe skim through it while sitting on the subway or bus. But let me share some of my experiences working as a doctor in a mission hospital in rural Zimbabwe, and maybe you too will wonder if I am on the same planet.

It's 7:30 in the morning and around the hospital you can hear singing and clapping as the different wards have their morning prayers. The enthusiasm with which the staff sing and the resulting harmonies start the day off on a beautiful and optimistic note.

As the singing finishes, I move on to hear the morning medical report. No admissions, no discharges and one death. These are the details in the report of the previous night for the pediatrics ward. A relatively good night, I think, remembering that my first night on call three children died. I know the patient who died last night: he was a nine-month-old boy named Fortunate whose mother had died the week before of AIDS.

Report ends and I start rounds on male ward. The ward is a big room divided into A and B sides. The official distinction between the two sides is that A are the acutely ill and post-operative patients, while B are the chronically ill patients. The distinction in my mind is that all the patients on B-side are HIV positive, or suspected to be, while only about half of A-side are.

Surprisingly, the healthiest patient on the ward is also the oldest: a 65-year-old with a hip fracture. This lucky man grew up in the generation before AIDS. Most of the other patients are around 30 years old, and they all have the "look:" the 40-kilogram, hollow-temples, skin-and-bones look. It is easy to forget that these are men in the prime of their lives. In a different time, or even today in a different country, they would be active young men—starting jobs and families. Instead they are struggling to keep food down, get to the toilet on time, and maintain any sense of dignity as they slowly waste away in the presence of their wives (those that are still alive), their parents, their children and the other patients who know their fate is similar.

I move on to the Outpatient Department, where a 27-year-old man has come to review his HIV test result. With pleasure I tell him it is negative. In fact, it is the first negative test I have seen since being here. He tells me that this is his third test this year. Surprised, I ask him why he has had so many. "Well, I'm thinking of doing some further education," he says, "but I'm not going to waste my time and money if I'm positive." I'm struck both by the bleakness of his statement and the reality it reflects. There is no way this hospital can afford to start any patients on anti-retroviral drug therapy.

My last patient of the morning is a 29-year-old man who, too weak to stand on his own, is wheeled in by his brother.

His wife is in confinement at another hospital, expecting their first child. Despite the language barrier I sense he is a strong man as he listens calmly. He smiles warmly when I ask if he knows whether his child will be a son or a daughter, in a desperate attempt to provide some positive note in this encounter. His brother, standing behind him, starts crying quietly as I bring up the possibility of HIV. I, too, mourn silently for this patient and for his unborn child ("a son" he has told me), who will likely never have the opportunity to meet his father. I finish and leave, emotionally exhausted, overwhelmed by the degree of suffering here, by the young ages of the patients and by the pervasiveness of this disease.

The next day, I head out on Home Based Care, a program that provides palliative care to AIDS patients. At each house, I am exposed to the far-reaching effects of HIV. At one, a grandmother cares for her soon-to-be orphaned grandchildren, as well as her dying 26-year-old daughter. At another, a three-year-old boy plays outside while his 24-year-old mother lies bed-bound in their hut. She is a strong woman, complains about nothing, thanks me despite the little I am able to offer her and smiles at me as I leave. Her mother, too, thanks us, and gives us a bag of maize. I wonder who will look after the AIDS orphans of the future, when this generation of healthy grandparents dies and their sons and daughters have already died before them.

As we drive home, I look out on the beautiful countryside, with its small, round huts surrounded by maize fields, the sun setting behind rocky outcrops, and people everywhere. I see men and boys herding cattle, girls carrying babies on their backs, women carrying loads of vegetables and fire wood on their heads or sitting by the roadside selling their produce. They all wave and smile as we pass by, the children often laughing and shouting out their hellos. This friendly, bustling environment seems a world away from the sadness that I know is a part of so many of their lives. I marvel at this happiness in the face of a disease that is tearing their homes, their families and their communities apart.

I believe that it is their joy in life that enables many of them to lead happy, fulfilled lives despite tragic circumstances. In our society, this culture of acceptance may seem foreign. In fact, naively, some may see it as a lack of initiative in dealing with the HIV problem, rather than a way of coping with a life that, even before AIDS, was far harder than anything most of us living in Canada could imagine.

I know from experience how easy it is to ignore, to be complacent, to just get caught up in our own lives. It is partly for this reason that I am writing about my experiences here. I hope for those of you who do think beyond your own existence, your own family and your own country that this will be a reminder of what is happening in Zimbabwe and other countries.

And for those of you who haven't thought about it— maybe you will.

*Eleanor Colledge*
Toronto, Ont.

# A SNOWY NIGHT IN BHUTAN

I was walking down our street in Ottawa's west end one night recently with my husband and our 10-year-old son. It was snowing.

The flakes fell slowly. Each tiny flake was a perfect crystal, all pointy and intricate the way snowflakes should be. These snowflakes weren't the tiny, nasty balls of ice that dig into your skin like needles. They were benign and beautiful, the type of snowflake that invites you to raise your face to the sky and ponder gravity.

In the world of human intercourse, I try to avoid gravity. I much prefer levity. But in the world of planets, moons, suns and galaxies, I recognize that gravity is what brings snowflakes to us. Having my son on hand and feeling like this might be a teachable moment, I asked him to think about the fact that gravity was pulling each of those snowflakes down to us, even though they seemed to be weightless. He didn't comment, he just looked up into the dark sky and pondered.

Back in the house, I settled down with a cup of tea and a large picture book on Bhutan, borrowed from the Ottawa Public Library. It's a book of stunning photographs taken by British photographer Tom Edmunds during two trips to

Bhutan. During the first trip, in 1996, he and his writer wife, Katie Hickman, rode donkeys and walked to the remote, eastern part of the country.

For most Canadians, all parts of Bhutan are remote. This tiny Himalayan kingdom, located just east of Nepal, is about the size of Lake Superior (if you smooth out the lake's jagged shoreline and create an oval out of its circumference). In self-imposed isolation from the rest of the world for most of its history, Bhutan is the world's last Buddhist state. Its historic and genetic ties to Tibet (with whom it shares a border) are strong. Who would have thought that, a half-century ago, China would re-assert control over Tibet, that the Dalai Lama would flee his country and that tiny Bhutan would be the standard-bearer for Vajrayana Buddhism in the Himalayas?

My interest in Buddhism and a meeting two summers ago with my husband's friend, Barun, who was born and raised in Bhutan, have sparked my interest in this country. Last fall, I enjoyed reading Hickman's *Dreams of the Peaceful Dragon: A Journey into Bhutan*. Some of Mr. Edmunds' photos appear in that book and, like any good spouse who admires her partner's work, Ms. Hickman unabashedly promotes her husband's solo publishing effort.

In mid-November, I decided I wanted to see Mr. Edmunds' pictures of Bhutan so I logged onto the Ottawa Public Library's website and reserved a copy of the book. Usually when I do this, the book I have ordered appears within two or three weeks. But in this case, almost two months passed before I got the call, in early January, that the book was in.

After we got home from our family walk in the snow the other night, I was lounging on our living room couch (as I am prone to do), my elbows digging into my torso in order to hold this coffee table book open in front of me. I was looking at pictures of a steep, forested slope in northern Bhutan, a mountainside iced with millions of snowflakes. Turning the page, my eyes were treated to the sight of running water in a black mountain stream. The banks of the stream and various stones in its middle were piled high with marshmallow gobs of snow, snow as smooth and white as the stream was smooth and black.

My husband caught sight of the photo and remarked on it. As I lifted the book higher, so he could see more clearly, I let go of one side of the book's cover. A small piece of white paper fell onto my chest. An imprint from a black rubber stamp proclaimed: Powassan Public Library. The top half of the word Public was not clearly visible, as happens when an official hand stamps a piece of paper impatiently. Handwritten in one corner, in blue ink, was this note: due Dec. 16/00.

Ah ha! Now, I knew why this book had taken so long to get to me. It had been on a journey to Powassan. Where's Powassan? my husband asked. Just south of North Bay on Highway 11, I told him. It's where our sister-in-law, who now lives in North Bay with my sister, was born and raised. That's why I know where Powassan is, I explained.

He seemed unimpressed with either my memory or my geographic savvy but I was pretty pleased with myself.

In fact, I felt warm and fuzzy for a couple of hours, knowing that someone in Powassan, Ont., had held this same picture book about Bhutan in their hands. The fact that this person (was she or he old or young, a student of geography or a refuge-taker in Buddhism?) had gone to considerable trouble to borrow my book through an inter-library loan made me feel connected, on a soul level, to a spirit on a path similar to mine. It felt like two snowflakes bumping into each other on their way to earth. And even though the snowflakes might dissolve the instant they hit the ground, I had the feeling that this kind of encounter, like being on the wheel of birth and death, was yet another miraculous manifestation of impermanence.

That night, it seemed to me, snow might be falling in Powassan, in Bhutan and in Ottawa.

*Debra Isabel Huron*
Ottawa, Ont.

# A CHRISTMAS IN AFGHANISTAN

It was 1970, the year Christmas wasn't supposed to happen. Newly married and graduated, my husband and I were off to see the world. And as the song said, there was such a lot of world to see. Our game plan to drive across Central Asia to India and points east was taking us farther away from family and friends with each flip of the odometer on the old blue Ford van. Across the mountains and deserts of Turkey and Iran, we were on the run from the familiar. We would spend Christmas in a land so remote and foreign that the microscopic organisms making up the homesickness virus could never find us. Skipping Christmas would be easy, in Afghanistan.

We crossed the frontier in mid-December. The highway, a black velvet ribbon built half by the Americans and half by the Soviets, was incongruously modern in a land that was anything but. I never got used to the sight of women shrouded head-to-toe in *burqas*, looking at the world through cotton bars from inside pastel gunnysacks. The men wore pantaloons, turbans and what looked to me like pointed Ali Baba shoes, but made from used tires. Passengers hung from the windows, jammed the rooftops and swung from the sides of psychedelic local buses. We were assured that as long as we didn't drive through the Khyber Pass after dark or approach the women, we would be safe. Afghanistan then was not the war-ravaged land of today, but it was still a very long way from middle-class Canada.

We checked into a 70-cent-a-night room at the Bezhad Hotel in Herat, where Hossain, the desk clerk, held sway. His official title didn't begin to do him justice. He was the ultimate concierge, friend and fixer to his itinerant clientele. Twenty-something (like most of the Bezhad's mainly Western patrons), Hossain took a long look across the cultural divide and seemed to like what he saw well enough. He was welcoming without feeling any need to understand us or figure us out, let alone explain us to ourselves.

"Me, I will never leave my home. Why would I?" He waited for an answer, but an acceptable one never came.

As Christmas neared, an idea so orthodox it was unorthodox percolated among the residents. We would put on a Christmas dinner as close to what we would have enjoyed at home, were we not so anxious to get as far away as possible as fast as we could from those same homes. The air was thick with equal parts nostalgia and irony. When we explained to Hossain why we wanted to borrow the hotel kitchen, he cocked his head and looked at us with fresh interest. So, we did come from somewhere, we did have roots. He grinned and offered to help in this feast for the Baby Jesus. We turned him down flat. As our guest of honour all he had to do was show up.

We should never have spurned the hand that knew best how to stoke the huge oven and keep it happy. We muddled through, slicing and dicing, baking and boiling, feeling more festive by the minute. We returned triumphant from the market with several scrawny chickens, turkeys not being an option. We were getting ready to set the tables when Hossain pulled the plug on us. With an uncharacteristically imperious wave, he barred us from the dining room. The threshold was not to be crossed without his say-so. We were too far into the big event to give up, but we now rolled out pastry and made gravy, sapped of most of our oomph. What had we done wrong?

Night fell before Hossain reappeared and ordered us to follow him. He stopped for a dramatic pause before flinging the dining-room doors open wide. We stared into the dark until slowly the soft light from dozens of candles bathed the cavernous room in amber.

"The stars, we bring them inside to you," Hossain beamed.

An apparition loomed in the far corner. Several hard squints and a leap of the imagination revealed seven men standing in tipsy formation, each propping up a bough from one of the area's scarce trees. A living Christmas tree if ever there was one! Hossain was puzzled when we were puzzled by branches covered in a coat of fresh paint. Christmas trees were supposed to be green, were they not?

Thirty of us sat down to dinner that Christmas night— Canadians, Americans, Trinidadians, Germans, Australians and those limbs of the tree not too shy to join us. We tucked into chicken, squash, potatoes, pumpkin pie and Christmas pudding. Between courses we stumbled through familiar carols. Hossain rose to make a toast.

"So many people like you come to Afghanistan today. You never speak of your home, as if you come from nowhere.

This year is different. You bring your Jesus Christmas to us. You show us you have a home. Thank you." He bowed and raised a glass of arak, gesturing around the table.

It was all too much for me. Blindsided by a sudden attack of homesickness, I burst into tears and ran from the room. A distraught Hossain was right on my heels. What had he done to offend? My ailment was explained. Hossain shook his head. The concept of homesickness was alien to him, but the solution was clear enough. Why didn't I go home? Why did I leave in the first place? I blubbered that I didn't want to go home, not then; I didn't want to be home, not yet; I just missed it. Hossain did the only sensible thing. He scratched his head and rejoined the party.

Thirty Christmases have passed since then. This year I will be away again, this time in England to celebrate the birth of my first grandchild, Rosie. Every year I think of Hossain. I hope that he is still alive. I hope that he never did have to leave his home. And I remember how he brought the stars to people foolish enough to think that leaving home was the same as forgetting it.

*Mary Preston*
Brockville, Ont.

## AN UNUSUAL CURE
## FOR THE WINTER BLAHS

No matter where you live in this great country of ours, any advertising having to do with travel at this particular time of year seems to hold an almost irresistible appeal. The multi-coloured posters and informational brochures that adorn all travel agency offices, along with solicitation through the media, exude a special warmth which touches our fancy and tends to inundate our thoughts with ideas of fun-in-the-sun somewhere other than where we are.

The temptation to succumb to the enticement of the people who sell the holiday excursions is what this kind of advertising is all about. Then, to complement all the various advertisements, we have the unsolicited testimony of sun-browned, smiling friends—completely satisfied winter vacationers—who have just returned from some simply wonderful place, some faraway land of utopian paradise, some Shangri-la where their dreams have been realized. This is the point where our innocent infatuation with the brochures can lead to a dangerous dalliance with the deadly sin of envy.

Now I can plainly understand why someone living in a smoggy, soggy, over-populated city would seek occasional respite from the winter on, shall we say, the beaches of Hawaii. Or perhaps on the coast of Mexico. And by simple reasoning I can clearly comprehend why those hardy souls habitually tolerating the long winter months on the frozen tundra of our Canadian Prairies (as I spent the first half of my life doing) might endeavour to temporarily transplant themselves to a balmier region a mite closer to the equator for a few weeks, at this time of year.

But I have, in the past, been given to wondering about people like myself, who live in the clement climes of Vancouver Island where the air is always stimulatingly fresh—usually due to an eclectic combination of wind and rain and sunshine—and where the temperature never strays too far below the zero mark, at least for any length of time. Why is it that we islanders seem to possess just as great a desire as most other Canadians to while away a few weeks of winter in some balmy setting either down south or down under or wherever? After some serious self-diagnosis, I determined that this yearly yen was probably due to an annual affliction that is quite common among us "wet coasters." For want of a better term, it's known as "the winter blahs."

This unsettling disorder, which is quite prevalent for several weeks on either side of the winter solstice, does, in fact, seem to affect inhabitants of our rather verdant back-yard to a greater degree than it does those denizens in other parts of our country where the variation of seasonal temperatures is more extreme. There is an obvious reason for this apparent phenomenon.

Anyone who has spent a full year or more in lotus land will notice that our seasons seem to blend into one another with relatively little fanfare. As a consequence, we simply become rather bored with it all. So, when winter comes along and the grey skies add to our state of ennui, our restlessness becomes an issue and we start making plans to escape to some reputedly pleasant place, some earthly Eden of our choosing, with the hope that we may ultimately find the cure for what ails us.

Unfortunately, with other priorities vying for our time and our money, many of us cannot always manage to fly away to tropical climes during the months of winter. So we either suffer out our winter blahs until the dawning of spring or we come up with some more convenient method of alleviating them. For all those of us who are currently caught in this rather common set of circumstances, I truly believe that I have found the ideal remedy.

The discovery of this cure was actually quite serendipitous rather than the outcome of some resolute scheme. A prerequisite is to purposely avoid all travel agencies and television advertising that attempts to whet my appetite for something different with pictures of aqua-coloured water washing up on white, sandy beaches.

Then I simply take a day or two and I go somewhere less pleasant than where I now live.

The nice part of it is, I usually don't have to go too far afield to find such a place. For instance, I have been known, on occasion, to hop a ferry and cross over the Georgia Strait to that rain-drenched and smog-infested metropolis that is commonly called the lower mainland; Vancouver to some. Not that I want to cast any aspersions on the city in which I was first introduced to the human race during the climax of the Second World War, but it is there that I am given the opportunity to lay myself open to the incessant drizzle of rain, to lend my ears to the ubiquitous roar of traffic and to yield my senses to the constant annoyance of crowds of people rushing from one place to another. They always manage to leave me with the distinct impression that they are late for some important appointment—probably the case with some of them but certainly not with all.

Perhaps there are those who would equate my somewhat unorthodox method of dealing with the winter blahs to the irrational actions of a person who beats his head against a wall so that he might savour the blissful feeling immediately after he stops. So be it. The important thing is, it works and it works well—for me at least. After patiently enduring the punitive experience of the big city for a given period of time, I most happily head back to my island sanctuary.

As the ferry I am travelling on rounds the final bend of the hour-and-a-half trip, I become aware that I have indeed left something behind on the mainland: my winter blahs.

*Garry Chartier*
Nanaimo, B.C.